JOHN F. FANSELOW
CONTRASTING CONVERSATIONS

ACTIVITIES FOR EXPLORING OUR BELIEFS AND TEACHING PRACTICES

Longman

To Kumiko
for the beginning and to
Aya Dorothy and Misa Laura
for the continuation

**Contrasting Conversations: Activities for
Exploring our Beliefs and Teaching Practices**

Copyright © 1992 by John F. Fanselow.
All rights reserved.
No part of this publication may be reproduced,
stored in a retrieval system, or transmitted
in any form or by any means, electronic, mechanical,
photocopying, recording, or otherwise,
without the prior permission of the publisher.

Longman, 95 Church Street, White Plains, N.Y. 10601

Associated companies:
Longman Group Ltd., London
Longman Cheshire Pty., Melbourne
Longman Paul Pty., Auckland
Copp Clark Pitman, Toronto

Distributed in the United Kingdom by Longman Group
Ltd., Longman House, Burnt Mill, Harlow, Essex CM20
2JE, England and by associated companies, branches,
and representatives throughout the world.

Executive editor: Joanne Dresner
Development editor: Elsa Van Bergen
Production editor: Andrea West
Cover design: Betty Sokol

The cloth pictured on the cover was purchased in Togo.

Library of Congress Cataloging in Publication Data

Fanselow, John F.
    Contrasting conversations: activities for exploring our beliefs
and teaching practices / John F. Fanselow.
        p. cm.
    Includes bibliographical references.
    ISBN 0-8013-0331-1
    1. English language—Study and teaching—Foreign speakers.
I. Title.
PE1128.A2F27   1992
428'.007—dc   20 91-37415
                                                            CIP

1 2 3 4 5 6 7 8 9 10 AL-95949392

CONTENTS

Foreword by Ann Lieberman vi
Acknowledgments vii

INTRODUCTION 1

Contrasting Approaches 1
The Power of Language 3
Learning Ways of Looking 4
The Workshop Approach 5
How This Book Works 6

PART ONE Learning to Look 9

THE GROUPING PROCESS 9

Invitation to Exploration 9
Grouping Stamps into Six Contrasting Pairs 9
Trying on a Different Lens 12
Fine-tuning Our Powers of Observation 17
Analyzing the Process of Looking 17
Your Perception of the World 18
Becoming Aware of the Effect of Filters 21
Building Perceptions 21
Recognizing Judgment 24
What Have We Learned about Looking? 26

RECONSTRUCTING OBSERVED LESSONS 28

Recording Observations 28
Seeking Different Representations of Reality 37
How We Select Affects What We Select 39

CONVERSATIONS ABOUT TEACHING: A REVIEW 42

Conversations Are Not Black and White 42
Looking at Our Own Conversations 46
Implications of Contrasting Conversations 50

PART TWO **Applications of Observing** 53

    Choices in Explorations   53

COMMUNICATIONS WITHOUT LANGUAGE   53

Unconscious and Conscious Communications   54
Analyzing Communications without Language   56
Adjusting Our Perceptions   58
How We Edit Our Observations   61
Noting Similarities and Differences   67
The Uses and Limits of Our Filters   69

FEEDBACK   72

The Many Meanings of "O.K."   72
Feedback Without Spoken Language   75
The Multiple Characteristics of Feedback   76
Trying Out Alternative Feedback   82
Does Our Feedback Reflect Our Beliefs?   83
Feedback as a Circle   86
Turning Feedback Upside Down   87

PATTERNS IN CLASSROOM TALK   89

Creating Space for Exploratory Talk   89
Exploratory Talk or Final Draft Talk—Doing a Flip-Flop   91
Altering the Proportion of Question Types   95
Communication as a Continuum   97

RECONSIDERING COMPREHENSION   98

Packaging Our Thoughts   98
The Limits of the Usual Conversations   103
One Person's Definition of Comprehension   105

RELATING THE CLASSROOM TO THE OUTSIDE WORLD   107

Bringing Outside Behaviors into the Classroom   107
Steps for Incorporating Outside Characteristics Inside a Class   108
Switching Places: Characteristics of Naming Tasks from the Learner's Point of View   114
Matching Intentions and Perceptions of Intentions   115
Questions as One Example of What a Teacher Does   116

SELECTING AND USING MATERIALS 118

Refreshing Our Vision 118
Designing a Class Setting 122
Summing Up the Beginning 127

STARTING CLASS 129

Ways of Greeting Students 129
Judging Ways of Greeting Students 131
Switching Approaches 132
Seeing Multiple Effects 132
Reaching Our Goals 135

TAKING STOCK OF OUR GOALS 139

The Range of the Things We Do 139
Re-examining Beliefs 143

WAYS OF NOTING RELATIONSHIPS BETWEEN DIFFERENT TYPES OF COMMUNICATIONS 148

A New Look at How We Communicate 148
Different Maps of Reality 153
Relating Classroom Communication to the Outside World 158

APPENDIX: OPTIONAL ACTIVITIES 161

BIBLIOGRAPHY 178

STAMPS 181

FOREWORD

In the vast literature on education, it is unfortunately rare to find books sensitive to the demanding work of teaching and, consequently, to the need for constant attention to its improvement and refinement. This attention, going beyond an "in-service day" or an occasional topic-specific workshop, takes forms that provide opportunities for teachers to reflect on their own understandings within the context of their own class and students. Because this central insight is still not well understood by those who are responsible for teacher improvement, effective programs for the development of teachers have, and continue to be, both obvious and illusive: obvious since everyone accepts the fact that teachers need continuous improvement and millions of dollars are spent working with new and experienced teachers telling them both what they should and should not do and illusive since the evidence suggests that too many pre- and in-service programs fail to make a difference to teachers' improvement. Perhaps this is because not enough people are sensitive to the amount of time it takes to both gain personal experience and learn from it, and aware of the support teachers need organizationally and personally to improve their own practice.

This book, written by a sensitive practitioner-scholar, begins to fill the gap between knowing *about* teacher development and knowing *how to* really engage teachers in their growth by using their own experiences in teaching. Fanselow knows that it is the teachers themselves who, with their colleagues, must become the primary shapers of their own development. He knows that whether they are brand-new or have years of experience, working together teaches teachers how to look at, critique, learn from, and improve their own teaching. He also knows how to create the learning opportunities to make this progress happen. The book is, as Fanselow suggests, a cookbook rather than a textbook. Within it is a particular kind of "cooking," from a chef with a well-seasoned approach to teacher development who is always explaining and deepening the lessons, and then pointing out new directions and ways of thinking. He engages teachers seriously and respectfully in observing each other, learning a language together to describe their teaching work, and talking about and providing the kind of encounters that allow self-knowledge to grow. What we learn as teachers is how to build professional knowledge while creating professional community with our colleagues.

This is the kind of teacher development that, through its sensitivity to and respect for the reality of teaching, can help to forge lasting improvements in its practice.

Ann Lieberman
Teachers College, Columbia University

ACKNOWLEDGMENTS

During and after workshops, teachers often ask me when I started to engage in the types of conversations I try to have about teaching. And they ask me who has been influential in my thinking and teaching. I normally respond by saying, simply, "I don't know." This is not the same as saying that I am not grateful to those I have worked with through the years; the comment simply indicates the fact that I find it difficult to pinpoint the people who have been most influential and the times when I developed one point of view or idea and another. Having said this, I feel compelled to state publicly the gratitude I feel to the many with whom I have come into contact in my years of professional work.

Teaching at a teacher training college in Nigeria in the Peace Corps, starting in 1961, provided one of the first opportunities for me to see viewpoints different from those with which I had previously been most familiar. My work there also compelled me to observe, since during practice teaching I was working with teachers who had from two to twenty more years of experience than I had. Fortunately for me there were two sections of each grade level at the schools where I visited practice teachers. I wrote copious notes indicating what the teacher in each section did and during our discussions I simply told each teacher at each grade level what the other teacher at the same level had done. This passing on of activities provided each teacher with additional resources. My role was simply that of a scribe and reporter. But the need to have something to tell the teachers gave me an impetus to observe quite precisely. The sixteen practice teachers I observed each term thus provided me with initial lessons for which I am very grateful.

During subsequent years, I had the opportunity to work with Americans bound for a number of countries in Africa and to observe many of them teach there, particularly in Somalia, Togo, and Senegal. To these American teachers, as well as the local teachers with whom we worked, I am very grateful. The preconceived notions that were turned inside out and upside down, day in and day out, by observations and conversations with both the teachers in these countries and their American guests is great in number.

In my work with Master of Arts candidates at Teachers College, Columbia University, both in New York and Tokyo, I have had countless opportunities to learn. I am very grateful to the scores of candidates I have worked with through the years, especially those who have tried some of the activities in this book and shared their reactions with me, such as William Casey, Laura Holland, Junko Inoue, Edward Mergel, Ines Modrcin, Yoko Murai, Midori Shimazaki, Matthew Taylor, Kazuko Unosawa, Atsuko Watanabe, and Setsuko Watanabe.

Most recently, in addition to working with teachers pursuing degrees, I have had the opportunity to work with teachers who are free from the conventions of students in degree programs. Through support from the Lowenstein Foundation, I was able to work with a group of teachers in Public School 42 in New York City. In spite of extra-heavy schedules, the teachers not only welcomed me into their classes but spent time with me during their breaks discussing their work and ideas. The principal, the late Anthony Barry, and those responsible for staff development, Rosemary Campbell and Victoria Rice, not only facilitated my visits but made me feel at home at their school.

Through the involvement of Barbara Agor at the Teacher Center in Rochester, New York, I have had the opportunity to learn from teachers trying many alternatives in that school district. These teachers include David Altobelli, Bonnie Dorschel, Linda Kantor, Warren Loeffler, Harold Messer, Cheryl Riley, Lillie Stone, and Nancy Sundberg.

For lending me their ears and their candor as they reviewed some of the activities or ideas in this book in earlier forms, I am most grateful to Paul Arcario, Mark Clarke, Craig Dicker, Sergio Gaitan-Flores, Jerry Gebhard, Steve Haber, Susan Keenan, Joan Lesikin, Virginia LoCastro, Ditte Lokun, Robert Oprandy, Stratton Ray, Mario Rinvolucri, Susan Stempleski, Naoko Tani, Daniel Tamulonis, Joyce Taniguchi, and Sihile Zwane.

In addition to observing others and asking others to listen, I teach. Understanding of my teaching has been deepened by co-teaching several times with Gay Brookes and Ray McDermott, so I must remind readers of their contribution to my ways of thinking as well.

To Eileen Zeidman, for nominating the article that formed the basis of this book for the Fred W. Malkemes Prize from the American Language Institute of New York University; and to Darlene Larson of the ALI, who has overseen this Award and been responsible for the initiation of many ways of recognizing teachers, I am very grateful. Awards for articles and books have a way of reminding us all of the value of written materials. The Bibliography section lists some of the printed materials that would constitute my nominations for awards.

In addition to people and materials that influence our thinking, there are those who make essential contributions to books. I am grateful to these people not only for the specific contributions I note here, but also for their insights: for transcripts, Kate Millet and Rob Walbridge; for photographs, Sandra McLean; for sketches, Misa Fujimura-Fanselow; for a drawing, John Emerzian; and for an incident reflecting preconceived notions, Michael Murphy.

Finally, no matter how many ideas I have gotten from the hundreds of teachers I have worked with, no matter how many people have listened to me and commented on what I have said and written, no matter how many endured earlier drafts of this book and made useful cuts and suggestions, not one page would have been printed without a publisher. Not only did Longman agree to publish this book of activities but fortunately for me, did so through Joanne Dresner and Debbie Sistino. They have made the development and publication of this book pure delight for me. The editor that they assigned to me, Elsa van Bergen, is the answer to every author's dream: a person who knows how to fulfill Robert Lewis Stevenson's plea: "to omit, to omit, if I only knew how to omit, I could make an *Iliad* of the daily newspaper."

Usually, the acknowledgment section ends with a statement by the author that the weaknesses in the material being discussed are entirely the responsibility of the author and not those who have been acknowledged. While I have no intention of blaming anyone for the shortcomings in this book, I must say that what I have written and the way I have written this book are inseparable from the influences of those I have worked with through the years.

INTRODUCTION

Once, during a practice teacher's lesson, I heard a supervisor shout: "You call yourself a teacher? I'll show you how to teach!" I was shocked. I was not shocked by the idea that one person could show another how to do something by presenting a short demonstration. Nor was I shocked by what seemed a judgment of the teacher's lesson. These elements—*advice* in the form of a demonstration and *evaluation* in the form of a seemingly negative judgment—are part of many post-observation conferences. Rather, I was shocked by the fact that the comments and subsequent demonstration occurred during a lesson in front of all the students, as well as some observing teachers like myself.

I was one of the only ones to be shocked, it turned out. As a matter of fact, the others in the room—observing teachers and the students of the class—had heard such comments made during lessons before, had seen demonstrations previously, and seemed used to both. Their understandings of the intentions, actions, and words of the speaker (or shouter) were different from mine. They were coming to this particular statement—"You call yourself a teacher? I'll show you how to teach!"—from a solidly established context of what I will call the "usual conversations" that emerge from observations of lessons.

CONTRASTING APPROACHES

The aims of the *usual conversations* that take place after an observation would be only slightly exaggerated if they were described as follows: "I am going to observe you and your actions and afterwards I will tell you what is right and wrong about your teaching and what needs to be improved. I will prescribe better activities or collaborate with you to develop better activities. Or if you have a problem, tell me, and I will help you solve it. I have been teaching a long time and know what will be needed to improve your performance as a teacher and to solve the problems I observe."

The usual post-observation conversations require one person to be in charge. The person in charge gives advice to a recipient in the form of suggestions or a demonstration to solve perceived problems. In contrast, in the kind of conversations encouraged by the activities of this book, neither the person observed nor the observer is in charge. With no one in charge autonomy and elbowroom are likely to be increased.

In the type of post-observation conversations that will emerge from the activities in this book, some evaluations will be replaced by descriptions and analyses of what is observed. Sometimes, cut-and-dried advice to solve a perceived problem will be replaced by *multiple interpretations* of what is observed. And the *exploration of relationships* between what is observed, what is said and done, and what had been intended will be carried out. With nothing to "prove" both participants can move freely, as

Introduction ■ 1

in play. Neither one is engaging in a power struggle where one gives advice to the other or evaluates and judges the other.

Without the need to wage a power play, both participants in the process of observation and discussion can see themselves more clearly—and can match what they say and do with what they think they are doing and saying, and with what they had hoped to do. They can match conscious and unconscious behaviors with intentions, teaching practices with beliefs.

I call these types of post-observation conversations *contrasting conversations* because they are different in some ways from the conversations in the usual post-observation conferences. I use "contrasting" in several ways. Among the meanings of *contrasting* is the suggestion of different, not better. Different means dissimilar, not new and improved or superior. *Contrasting* also suggests the value of conversations in which each participant presents a viewpoint different from the one each usually presents. To the extent that such conversations are uncommon, *contrasting* also suggests unusual as juxtaposed to usual. The conversations that grow out of the activities in this book are frequently very different from those teachers regularly have; *contrasting* also refers to this fact.

The description, comparison, and analysis that take place during contrasting conversations require that we listen to other points of view. But they also require us to appreciate other points of view and suspend judgment. They require us to sometimes say: "I'm going to try that. Even though I don't yet see any value in it, since you have found some value in it, I want to at least explore it."

The aims of these contrasting conversations might be described as: learning ways of looking as a means to expand our repertoire of teaching practices; discovering something about our beliefs and teaching practices that we have not seen before; being freed to try teaching practices that others, or even ourselves, have judged inadequate; becoming more aware of our beliefs and the ways they can control the range of our teaching practices; using evaluations of teaching practices to explore our beliefs rather than to judge them, and to free us to try alternatives rather than to prescribe.

Comments introducing the aims of the contrasting conversations that I hope will emerge from the activities in this book might go like this:

> I am going to observe you. Afterwards, when I look at excerpts from your lesson with you, I hope that through the analysis—playing with the words we use to discuss the lesson—we can see something we did not see before about our own teaching. Jointly comparing similarities and differences between your teaching practices and beliefs and my teaching is likely to reveal multiple interpretations of what we described. Let's explore teaching together!

> I came to your class not only with a magnifying glass to look carefully at what was being done, but with a mirror so that I could see that what you were doing is a reflection of much of what I do.

Using the patch of cloth shown on the cover and the stamps reproduced in the back of this book and below in the same way that we'd use transcriptions or notes made from a classroom visit, the usual conversation about them, emphasizing evaluation, would sound like this:

> The centering of the 5-cent Pocahontas stamp (#9) is not good at all. The amount of selvage is not even on each side, so it's like an uneven frame around a picture. If the centering were better and if the selvage were wider all around, it would be worth much, much more. As it is, it is run of the mill and not worth adding to most collections. The two figures in the patch of cloth are done with fine craftsmanship.

The contrasting conversations that emerge from the activities in this book would emphasize description, comparison, and analysis and sound like this:

> The designs above the heads of the two figures in the piece of cloth on the cover are similar in some ways to the hat Pocahontas is wearing in the 5-cent Jamestown stamp. I hadn't noticed the hat before; there seem to be similar designs in the stamp and the piece of cloth; look at the patterns on the cloth jacket Pocahontas is wearing and the designs on the smaller figure in the cloth. At first, the hat attracted my attention, and I did not see the face. But now I see how the hat, perhaps by seeming out of place, draws attention to Pocahontas's face.

THE POWER OF LANGUAGE

Conversations, communication, and teaching itself depend, of course, on language. Much of our lives is spent in trying to match both our own and others' understandings of words, intentions, and actions. It is said that Stanislavski, the famous Russian director, required those he auditioned to utter only two words: "Good evening." Those who uttered the words to express the greatest variety of meanings were given parts. "Good evening" said to a doorman, for example, means something different from "Good evening" uttered by a young man to a young woman as they meet for their first date. In discussing our teaching practices, understanding the uses and implications of language is crucial. Such understanding can be aided by matching and rematching understandings of words ("not quite" after a student's error), actions (a frown after the same error), and intentions (stopping the learner from making the error).

Across the centuries various scholars have grappled with the phenomenon of language—its pitfalls and its potentials. Bakhtin, a Russian literary scholar and philosopher whose work from the 1920s has recently become influential, pointed out that language is not a fixed, abstract system but depends on the speaker's perception of the world:

> All words have the "taste" of a profession, a genre, a tendency, a party, a particular work, a particular person, a generation, an age group, the day and hour. Each word tastes of the context and contexts in which it has lived its socially charged life: all words and forms are populated by intentions . . . language, for the individual consciousness, lies on the borderline between oneself and the other. The word in language is half someone else's. . . . Language is not a neutral medium that passes freely and easily into the private property of the speaker's intentions; it is populated—overpopulated—with the intentions of others. Expropriating it, forcing it to submit to one's own intentions and accents, is a difficult and complicated process.
>
> (Bakhtin, 1981, pp. 293, 294)

We tend to forget that observation and post-observation conversations are part of a process involving both participants. The challenge of putting this realization to work for each of us is an exciting one. Out of our contrasting conversations can come a creativity that can evolve from joint exploration. An excerpt from the Socratic dialogs reveals the essence of both genuine exploration and joint learning, and perhaps, a bit of playfulness:

> SOCRATES: . . . for I perplex others, not because I am clear, but because I am utterly perplexed myself. And now I know not what virtue is, and you seem to be in the same case, although you did once perhaps know before you touched me. However, I have no objection to join with you in the enquiry.
>
> from *The Meno*

Language, then, can constrain us, or it can be used consciously to set us free. The activities of this book are expressly designed to free us in our observing, our thinking, and our teaching practices. Rather than saying something such as "I can't let the students hand out the materials themselves, they will get out of control," you might feel ready to say "I'm not sure what will happen if I let the students hand out the materials themselves, so I will let them and see what happens." As you will be reminded from time to time throughout the book, there are no right answers, no expected solutions in the activities.

LEARNING WAYS OF LOOKING

One goal of the conversation we usually find as part of post-observation is to learn ways of teaching. One goal of the contrasting conversations that will emerge from the activities in this book is also to learn ways of teaching. But we will discover that ways of teaching are learned as part of the larger goal of learning ways of looking. Learning how to teach by learning how to look enables us to continue to explore our teaching, to continue to try, discard, and retry alternatives that we discover.

The activities you choose to do will expand your capacity for learning ways of looking. And this in turn will enable you to experience the act of creating your own knowledge. Such creations might enable us to become more responsible for our decisions and our lives.

THE WORKSHOP APPROACH

As an important matter of fact, this book is not a package of information nor a traditional text but rather a workshop with a variety of activities to choose from. The activities are not the ends but the means to the end of illustrating ways of looking and of having contrasting conversations. Your dialogs will be what move you past language that is "half someone else's" to different understandings of words and to explore relationships between intentions and actions, between beliefs and teaching practices.

In other words, this book offers a technique. It focuses on consciously matching words with actions and intentions in a range of ways, and in a spirit of playfulness that can reveal how we each mean something different by the same term or the same thing by different terms. The words we use to discuss teaching practices can be compared to words in any other setting. What does the parent's "Knock the egg gently against the side of the bowl" mean to a child the first time the child and parent are scrambling eggs together? Just as "bowl" is uttered, the child smashes the egg against the bowl. After a few matchings between intentions and actions and words, the child and parent often understand "knock," "gently," and "bowl" in a different way. (They might also have a big laugh about the eggs.)

Without a conscious description and analysis of what we do, multiple interpretations of exchanges from lessons, and an exploration of teaching, our conversations about our teaching will continue to be intuitive, imitative, and informal, whereas they could be informal *as well as* technical, explicit, and analytical.

The words "technical" and "analytical" sound cold and lifeless to many people, and even threatening to some, while "informal" sounds warm and cozy. Yet I use "technical" to suggest a practical, applicable technique, which can work along with intuition. The term "analytical" brings us to a key concept in this book, the use of *grouping* into categories of characteristics in order to reveal what was not seen before. Artists, inventors, explorers, authors, and musicians use analytical skills to group and regroup elements of their craft; they toy with ideas, and they exhibit the playful spirit that informs this book. Using technique, therefore, does not have to be cold or lifeless. The cloth on the cover and the stamps shown in this book required intuition as well as technique and exploration.

The technique does not have to be time-consuming either. The activities that produce contrasting conversation are based on the premise that a few exchanges or activities can reveal a great deal.

For the teacher or supervisor who wants to learn how to teach by being shown ways of teaching through prescriptions and models, there are scores of methods books available, to say nothing of the teachers' notes that accompany almost all textbooks. The hundreds of suggestions in these books provide more than enough prescriptions, as well as implicit and explicit criteria for evaluating teaching. It is not that I avoid prescriptions. I give a number of prescriptions in this book. But those prescriptions are given to provide: alternatives for comparisons; options for exploration; and a means of providing teaching practices to try in your teaching that will aid you in learning different ways of looking.

HOW THIS BOOK WORKS

This "workshop" centers on activities to be done with a partner. Part One focuses on the process of looking, and, to open your mind to possibilities, we begin with activities that would seem to have little to do with teaching per se. They are, however, what starts us off in the process of looking and exploring our beliefs and teaching practices. By the end of Part One we will be able to use certain new skills or techniques as teachers and observers.

Part Two applies what we have learned about looking to a range of classroom situations and activities. There is no need to follow the sequence of topics of Part Two as listed in the table of contents, which is simply alphabetical. Some sections of Part Two deal with what some might consider tangential topics, such as taking attendance, while others cover areas basic to any discussion of teaching. Given the aim of learning how to teach through learning how to look, any topic can be dealt with because the process of looking is central rather than the specific subject of the topic. In other words, there is no presupposition that exploring different ways of starting class or selecting materials will necessarily yield less information about how to teach than exploring "comprehension" or another such educational topic: The presupposition is that all of our topics are interrelated. Thus, a small change in the way we greet students might affect how we deal with comprehension in a profound way. It is in the classroom as it is in the ecology of the world outside: Diverse forms of life and activity are interrelated and interdependent. For example, a slight increase in the number of cattle that graze in a dry area can increase the rate of erosion in geometric proportions.

You will be asked in both Part One and Part Two to have not only a partner and a pencil or pen (and for some activities, colored pencils) but some sort of taping equipment also. For several of the activities audiotape is sufficient. You should also arrange to record, preferably on videotape, short excerpts from classes and then transcribe parts of them.

The Purpose of Grouping Activities

As mentioned, this book utilizes the technique of grouping. In the process of grouping, you and your partner will often arrive at common meanings for terms by constant comparison between items you have selected and categorized and the labels you have assigned these groups.

After excerpts from lessons are grouped on the basis of the single dimensions represented by the categories you create, you can regroup them so that different dimensions of the same excerpts can be seen. As you match the labels for the groupings with excerpts that fit the groupings, you will see how the words we use to describe our teaching practices reflect our beliefs—our preconceived notions about good and bad teaching. And you will also see how frequently the meaning you assign to a term and how your partner understands the meaning of that term are totally different (as well as how frequently you each use different terms to refer to the same phenomenon).

As you realize that the terms we use are often less important than the beliefs our teaching excerpts represent, you can compare your feelings about labels with others. This is an important task.

Dialogs in which we describe and analyze are important, but without action they are insufficient. As you see different characteristics of teaching practices in classes and discuss them, I will invite, request, or prescribe a change in some practice in a subsequent class. The change will emerge from some of the classroom excerpts that have been analyzed. Often, the changed practice will simply require the introduction of something that is the opposite of what was found in the first analysis. For example, if a neutral comment such as "So, so" was made after incorrect student responses, a negative comment such as "No" will be prescribed. After I invite, request, or prescribe a variation of one small segment of your teaching, I will show you ways to explore the multiple results of the different options you try. One way of doing this is to consider results and practices you consider negative in a positive way, and vice versa. For example, if you consider teacher enthusiasm positive, I'll ask you to list two or three disadvantages of teacher enthusiasm.

The dialogs you will have with your partner, and with yourself, and the various alternatives you will use in your teaching are not the ends, but the means to understanding your teaching and to discovering new ideas. By constantly considering practices and results you consider negative in a positive way, and vice versa, your beliefs about their values will change. You will learn how to compare options in new ways.

When you and your partner turn previous interpretations of teaching excerpts upside down and inside out, you are likely to see some feature of teaching you did not previously see, thus producing new knowledge. As you engage in contrasting conversations, you will be able to react to a range of claims, such as that of the Brazilian educator Freire's observation: "Knowledge emerges only through invention and re-invention, through the restless, impatient, continuing, hopeful inquiry [people] pursue in the world, with the world, and with each other." (Freire, 1970, p. 58)

The discussions that usually grow out of classroom observations based on judgments and prescriptions, on "I'll show you how to teach!," often provide a type of certainty that the explorations and descriptions in the contrasting conversations that grow out of the activities in this book hopefully will not. The conversations that emerge from the activities in this book will likely contain comments that show movement from firmly held positions to floundering uncertainty; some comments will probably reflect confusion.

But according to many who have done the activities before you, it is from such constant questioning of the meanings of what we do and from trying out alternative practices that different types of certainty develop. There is the certainty that we can learn about what we do, and the certainty that we can use judgments we and others make to explore our beliefs and teaching practices rather than to evaluate them.

How to Use This Book

The activities of this book have been used in both regular courses, attended by those who have never taught before and those who have from 1 to 35 years experience, and in workshops for teachers, mentors, or supervisors. You will find this book—workshop—applicable in a variety of situations. If you are in a methods class and looking for a project that includes exploration of your beliefs and teaching practices, you could work through portions of this book with a classmate. If you are currently teaching and feel the need for a fresh perspective, as we all do from time to time, try working through units of this book with a colleague. If you teach a course in observation, methods, or supervision, you could ask some students in the class to try out a section or an activity and report back to the group. If you supervise teachers or are serving as a cooperating teacher or teacher mentor for the first time, you could use a section or two to begin contrasting conversations with the teacher you are working with. No matter what your starting point, you are likely to discover something different about your beliefs and teaching practices and about your interactions with others outside of class. You will probably see much of what you have been looking at for years in a different way.

Given the tight schedules most of us have, observing other teachers—let alone engaging in contrasting conversations—might seem an impossible undertaking. But the individual activities in this book can be done by those with limited time. Each activity takes from only 5 minutes to an hour to complete, depending on how much you and your partner talk. (Though the activities are planned to be done jointly, they can, of course, be done alone. In this case, you would play two roles.)

Collecting the teaching excerpts you need for the activities in each section need not be very time-consuming either, since the excerpts required are short. I advocate using classroom observations of a minute or less in most activities.

The bulk of the time in each activity is devoted to grouping and interpreting data, not collecting data. Of course, seeing only a minute or two of a lesson prevents us from seeing lesson development. But it provides a great deal to analyze. In many classes, thirty questions are asked in a minute, and more than a dozen instances of feedback can be seen in 60 seconds as well. In a full class period, hundreds of communications are made, each in a split second. Consequently, trying to describe and analyze more than a minute or so in any kind of detail is an almost impossible task.

The activities in each section are designed to be completed over time, doing one or two activities at a time, limiting a meeting with a colleague to a half hour or so. They are not designed to be completed in one marathon session. Time off for reflection between activities is important.

Consider this book more like a cookbook than a textbook, more an anthology of poems than a novel, to be dipped into and used intensely for short periods of time rather than gone through from beginning to end in a short period of time.

Though it is vital to find some time to be physically together with a partner to do the activities, many of them can be discussed on the telephone or through computer mail. As long as each person in the pair or group has the same data, the joint analysis and interpretation of the data can still be accomplished.

PART ONE   # Learning to Look

THE GROUPING PROCESS

INVITATION TO EXPLORATION

Through the ages human beings have explored in order to discover something not yet seen, and to learn. Bronowski, a scientist who was devoted to showing connections between scientific and artistic creations, summed up the real purpose of the work at hand:

> The discoveries of science, the works of art are explorations—more, are explosions—of a hidden likeness.... When a simile takes us aback and persuades us together, when we find a juxtaposition in a picture odd and intriguing, when a theory is at once fresh and convincing, we do not merely nod over someone else's work. We re-enact the creative act, and we ourselves make the discovery again....
> The habit of testing and correcting the concept by its consequences in experience has been the spring within the movement of our civilization.... In science and in art and in self-knowledge we explore and move constantly by turning to the world of sense to ask, Is this so? This is the habit of truth, always minute yet always urgent.
>
> (Bronowski, 1956, pp. 19, 46)

Grouping is a technique that produces those "intriguing juxtapositions." It thus engages us in the process of exploration and discovery. We will begin with a grouping activity that asks you to look freshly at objects we all take for granted.

In the back of this book you will find black-and-white reproductions of postage stamps. To put grouping into practice you could use different versions of any kind of item. But if we all work with postage stamps at this point, we will have common ground for our conversations.

GROUPING STAMPS INTO SIX CONTRASTING PAIRS

Before You Begin

Throughout this book you will be presented with a number of options, of "reader's choice" situations. For example, you may choose to skip a certain activity that someone else may wish to do or do differently than you.

Your first option concerns the manner of actually doing the grouping. Some people feel they sort visually: They look at an image, mentally sort it into a category, and find a way, by a description or identifying number, to list the image as part of that category. If that is your choice, cut out the whole page for easy viewing as you do the activities. Others like to sort tactilely. If you are one of them, you can cut apart the stamps so you can move them around and actually see juxtapositions; but leave the identifying numbers with the stamps.

Activity 1

With a colleague, group the postage stamps reproduced in the back of this book into six contrasting pairs. First, decide upon a specific basis of comparison/contrast. One example of a feature to use in grouping, or categorizing, would be shape or format: There are (a) stamps that are horizontal, and (b) stamps that are vertical. Use the worksheet that follows to list your selections by number or description (such as Lincoln or Pocahontas, #5 or #9), or place the images under each category, writing the titles of each group at the top of each column in the "T." There must be at least two stamps under each column, and all of the stamps must be categorized. There are no right or wrong answers!

Try to come up with the six pairs of words in a short amount of time. What does "short" mean? Three minutes? Thirteen? Thirty? Each person's *short* is, of course, different. And time is also relative: 30 minutes at one task seem like 3, and at another 3 seem like 30. Note when you begin and end. Does it seem a short amount of time to you and to your colleague?

If at all possible, tape the exchanges between youself and your partner as you group the stamps. Later, it will be easier to describe and analyze some features of the conversations you have and to see the extent to which they contrast with other types of conversations you commonly engage in. When you are finished with the activity, stop your tape recorder, and write "grouping stamps" or some other label on the tape.

10 ■ Learning to Look

Thinking about the Alternatives

Compare your titles with titles that others generated. So you can more easily see features others noticed and you and your partner did not, cross out any titles you have in common.

Here are some of the possible contrasting pairs:

odd numbers	even numbers
transportation	no transportation
globes	no maps or globes
with dates	without dates
digits in circles	digits not in circles
"U.S. Postage" on top	"U.S. Postage" on bottom
5 cents	more or less than 5 cents
with routes traced on them	without routes traced

(continued on next page)

numbers on the bottom	numbers on the top
numbers only in Arabic script	numbers written out in words
Gothic lettering	Roman lettering
pictures of scenes framed	pictures of scenes not framed
historical events or people	things and general scenes
air mail	non-air mail
clouds	no clouds

By asking you to provide words to describe groups in these activities, you are not being set up. The point of the activities is *not* to get you to reveal your ideas and then show you how silly or how different they are from the ones I cite. Remember, *there are no wrong answers possible in this book!*

The only thing that is required in doing the grouping in this book is to compare your answers with those of others. If you are willing to play with the ways you look at things—and at your teaching—and are then willing to play with your teaching methods, you will learn how to teach in a way no other person can show you.

TRYING ON A DIFFERENT LENS

While there are no correct answers, it is true that many people who work at grouping these stamps produce many of the same categories. This suggests that we have preconceived notions about postage stamps that lead us to see certain of their features, just as we have preconceived notions that lead us to say "enthusiastic" or "helpful" about teachers or "disrespectful" about students. But appealing as an enthusiastic teacher might seem to be, noting some disadvantages of enthusiasm can lead us to see how such a belief can be limiting as well as useful.

Teacher enthusiasm may overwhelm some students who tend to be quiet even among other quiet peers. Or, if a teacher shows more enthusiasm for some topics than others, which seems inevitable, the students may begin to think that what the teacher is most enthusiastic about is most important. Thus, if a history teacher is enthusiastic mainly about dates and battles, for example, the students might believe that people or issues are not significant in history. The enthusiasm toward the content of history, if not balanced with enthusiasm for students, might also seem to some students misplaced; some might wonder why the teacher does not show more interest in their personal histories or in them as people. Unless those of us who believe in the value of enthusiasm try being unenthusiastic about what we are normally enthusiastic, and vice versa, we cannot understand the limitations and values of either enthusiasm or restraint.

In the same way, though we might think that giving a student an answer is helpful, other interpretations need to be considered. Is giving the answer a signal to the student that we don't think he or she can produce the answer? Is giving an answer signaling impatience with students, who, learning something for the first time, may need longer to respond than those who know the answer? Some children in the park can be heard saying "Let me do it alone, Dad; I can do it; don't help me!," signaling another possible understanding of "helpful."

Believing that students who wear hats in school show disrespect can prevent us from considering the possibilities that some students might wear hats to feel identified with a group, or because they are embarrassed about head size or hair. Assuming that student giggling always means disrespect prevents us from considering the possibility that giggling can signal nervousness and shyness, among other things.

Activity 2

To clearly demonstrate how our range of preconceived notions limits what we see, now try grouping in a different way. On the worksheet that follows are listed a number of category titles not used previously. Think of each title you did not use as a different lens through which you can view the stamps.

With a partner, discuss which stamps fall under the various column titles—analyze what features the different lenses reveal that the lenses you used before did not. This time, use a different sorting method, too. If you sorted visually before, try doing it tactilely.

Notice that there is space on the top of the last two columns for you to add labels to describe features you notice that the other column titles do not highlight. In this activity there are no right or wrong, no superior or silly column titles, but there are some right answers regarding where you would assign any given stamp.

If you choose, you may select only a few column titles you find particularly difficult to assign stamps. Tape record your sorting conversation if at all possible.

1. *patriotic symbols* 2. *water*

3. *flora—trees, flowers, leaves, grains* 4. *sources of heat*

5. *have words that are not necessarily English*

6. *your title:* 7. *your colleague's title:*

Thinking about the Alternatives

With this activity we have progressed in our exploration together from looking and labeling to more analytical perception. What follows attempts to capture the essence of conversations that could have emerged from this second activity. You will, I expect, quickly note that there are almost as many questions as there are statements.

1. *Patriotic Symbols.* Some of the categories suggested usually produce more agreement than others. The fact that all the stamps are from the United States raises the question of whether some of these patriotic symbols are used by other countries or whether all the symbols on these

stamps can be patriotic symbols only for the United States. The flags on stamp #5, the 5-cent Lincoln, are considered patriotic symbols by most, and some put Lincoln himself down as a patriotic symbol, so count #5 twice. The shields beneath the "5" on each side of Pocahontas in #9 and the 5-cent Jamestown (#13) are patriotic symbols to some, whether they are from the United States or not, since shields are patriotic symbols in many places.

Is Old Faithful, in #6, the 5-cent Yellowstone, a patriotic symbol? The white cloudlike shape on this stamp reminds some of an atomic bomb explosion—a tragic patriotic symbol, many have said. The head in #10, the 5-dollar America, is commonly noted as a symbol. Since the eagle has been a patriotic symbol in many countries from Roman times to the present, #11, the 6-cent air mail stamp, is regularly placed in this category. The document illustrated in #13, which shows the signing of the compact or agreement providing for the temporary government of the Plymouth colony, is considered patriotic by those who know of the event. Many ask: Where would the American form of government be without the Mayflower Compact, which created the first American settlement based upon a social contract?

If you are not native to the United States, you may say that these stamps and such patriotic symbols are foreign to you. It should be noted that most people from the United States come to these stamps also for the first time, since none of those reproduced have been used for postage in more than 50 years. Of course, the Pilgrim compact as well as Freeman's exploration of California and the founding of Jamestown might still be more familiar to those from the United States, because of history classes. But by trying to take off our "I can't group items from a different country lens," it might be possible to see more patriotic symbols than citizens of the United States, who might be so familiar with some items that they miss seeing them.

Determining which items are patriotic symbols does not only involve the patriotic symbols themselves, but similarities and differences between each person's interpretation of what is a patriotic symbol. Is Lindbergh's plane, which now hangs in a museum in the capital of the United States, any sort of patriotic symbol? Is Byrd's expedition? Are the mayflower plants on the sides of #13, or the hold of the ship, the *Mayflower*?

In our conversations about teaching, we need to ask these kinds of questions if we are really determined to see what others see and to compare our meanings with theirs. Each must cite multiple examples of a student response that is seen as engaging or stimulating, otherwise the meanings of the words are not precise. For example, one person observing student responses to the following questions thought the students were engaged, while another thought the students were simply answering questions both they and the teacher already knew the answers to.

> TEACHER: How many millimeters equal 1 centimeter?
> STUDENTS: 10, 10, 10!
> TEACHER: If you times it by 2, what will you get?
> STUDENTS: 20 millimeters! 20! 2 centimeters?
> TEACHER: O.K. Now, I'll ask you to times it by 10 and what do you get?

STUDENTS: (silence, moving around in seats)

TEACHER: (Holds up a meter stick) Who can remember what this equals?

STUDENTS: 100—a hundred! Yeah, 100!

TEACHER: If I had 3 meters—3 sticks like this—how many centimeters would I have?

STUDENT 1: 300.

TEACHER: How did you get that?

STUDENT 1: You count them?

STUDENT 2: You can add 100 plus 100 plus 100.

STUDENT 3: How 'bout multiplying? 3 times 1?

After applying the "knew answers to the question" lens, the observer who thought the students were engaged reconsidered and noticed that only the last question and the final student response required any thought or engagement of the students. And the observer with the "knew answers to the question" lens, after trying on the "students engaged" lens, noticed both that the final question required more than answers the students knew and that even the question "If I had 3 meters—3 sticks like this—how many centimeters would I have?" was different from the previous questions. So, both saw something new by trying each other's categories. In the same way, in grouping the stamps, what is seen as patriotic to some in the United States may be seen as chauvinistic to others and exploitative to others.

2. *Water.* In this category we could certainly put the Atlantic Ocean depicted on #1, the 10-cent Lindbergh, and the oceans in the globes in #2, the 3-cent Byrd Antarctic, as well as the bodies of water in the globe in #3, the $2.60 Zeppelin, and #7, the 5-cent Olympic commemorative. What of the water Columbus seems to have beneath his ship in #4? And if the water *under* a ship, then what of the water outside the ship in #13, the 5-cent Pilgrim Tercentenary? The ship is not in dry dock on shore; should it be grouped in the category called *water*? And what of the clouds in #8, the 5-cent Fremont? In #6, Old Faithful in Yellowstone produces steam—water in another form.

Of course, the goal of the grouping is not to prove a point but rather to see a point that you might have otherwise missed without looking through the lenses, labels, or preconceived notions of others. With the caption "Columbus in sight of land" in #4, water does not come to everyone's mind. But when asked to look for water in each stamp, which is what categorizing in pairs forces us to do, we might notice what previously we had not seen. Working through these activities is something like mental gymnastics, keeping the mind toned and flexible enough for contrasting conversations and an awareness of the alternatives and similarities inherent in any situation.

3. *Flora.* The mayflower plants on #13 quickly come to our attention once we are focusing on plant forms as do the leaves around the head in #10. The grain above the vignette in #8 and the ears of corn beneath it are seen by some only when they see the word *grain* after flora in the column title; *flora* does not itself provide the lens that reveals the ears of corn.

Some assume that there have to be some plants on the Rocky Mountains so they placed #8 under flora. The acanthus leaf above each of the 5s in #10 are not often noticed. Searching for plants leads some to claim that there are trees on the shore Columbus seems to be looking at in #4. Some argue that there are trees, or at least small plants around Old Faithful in #6.

4. *Sources of Heat.* Some insist that the engines in the Lindbergh plane in #1, the Zeppelin in #3, and the biplane in #12 produce heat. Some contend that Pocahontas must be warm with her clothing on, as shown in #9, and that the discus thrower in #7 must be warm even without clothing, since he is exerting so much energy. Old Faithful produces hot water, so some put #6 in this column. The flames on the two torches in the 5-cent Olympic stamp (#7) do not seem to stand out and so are missed by some.

5. *Have Words That Are Not Necessarily English.* This grouping often draws out more controversy than the others. Though *Zeppelin* in #3 was the name of a German designer of lighter-than-air airships, the name is used in English as well as many other languages, so is it German or English plus something else? *Graf* is German for *count*, but in this context is it German only? *Pocahontas* in #9 is an Indian name but is used by English speakers, so is it English? *Olympiad* (#7)? What language is that? And what about *Los Angeles* in the same stamp? What if laws in English-speaking countries mandate that only English be used? Must we stop using names that are not English? What makes a word English?

Note that the categories *patriotic symbols*, *water*, *flora*, *sources of heat*, and *non-English words* not only highlighted features we considered different, they also provided us with a means to see similarities between stamps we had not previously noticed. For example, few at first group the stamps with clouds (#2, #3, #7, and #12) together with the Atlantic Ocean in #1. Fewer still think of water when they look at Columbus on the deck of his ship and the Pilgrims in the hold of their ship. The sweat some attribute to the discus thrower and Pocahontas further highlight the similarities between stamps that on the first few viewings seem to have nothing in common.

In fact, once the categories are viewed as a means to seeing similarities, it can be claimed that Lincoln (#5) must have been as hot as Pocahontas when he was sitting to have his picture taken. And so maybe he was sweating also. And the leaves surrounding America's head (#10) needed water to develop and no doubt now contain water since they do not appear dry. In short, by looking at the seemingly contrasting categories, similarities rather than differences can be seen. Consequently, we can move beyond the usual way of grouping so common in our day-to-day stereotyping of much that we observe. Thus, we group not only to determine how items are different but how seemingly different items have underlying or "hidden likenesses," to borrow Bronowski's words. Conversely, in the same process we often see differences between items that at first seemed the same.

I hope that as you and your partner grouped the stamps, your disagreements about matching certain stamps to certain words led to more than just a struggle with the verbal skills you used to package your ideas. As you wondered whether you should change some of the labels I provided because a word such as flora was, say, too broad, or too technical, perhaps you experienced what Arnheim, who writes about visual thinking, calls the "true drama going on in thought." Maybe you were able to "see things in a new light" and realized that the adjustment of the language to the "new insight is nothing more than a bothersome technicality." (Arnheim, 1969, p. 246)

Optional Activity: Additional Practice with the Grouping Process

My prevailing hope is that you will find this book responsive to your needs, interests, and pace. If you and your partner would like to work with still other categories of stamp grouping, turn to Activity 2A in the appendix to this book. If not, go on to Activity 3.

FINE-TUNING OUR POWERS OF OBSERVATION

> When I watch the way people record their observations of lessons I have noticed that fewer people draw sketches than write words. Some people contend that sketching and drawing activate a different part of the brain than does writing words.
>
> (Edwards, 1979, p. 4)

Activity 3

To encourage development of your powers of observation, color two or three of the black-and-white reproductions of the stamps, using well-sharpened colored pencils. While coloring pictures is of course different from sketching, it seems more similar to the tasks involved in sketching than to those involved in writing notes.

Your coloring of the stamps forces you to focus on details. For example, some people notice the child in the 1-cent Columbus (#4) for the first time when they use different colors for coloring separate figures. When you realize what you might have missed, you may have a greater appreciation of the value of drawing sketches of body language, locations of students, interactions, objects used, and so forth during classroom observations.

After you have colored a few stamps, compare your coloring with another person's. Do you now see details not noticed in the previous grouping activities? More importantly, do you sense more clearly the different individual perceptions of reality we impose on objects and situations?

ANALYZING THE PROCESS OF LOOKING

Before we turn to grouping and thinking about observed lessons, take advantage of the "neutral ground" of stamp grouping to analyze the tasks of looking. I have suggested a number of activities to help focus your thinking.

Activity 4

Using the lines below, write your comments about the different types of grouping you have used so far. For example, the method of sorting—visual or tactile—might have affected the way you grouped the stamps. What was the difference between using your eyes alone and using your eyes with your fingers and hands? What reactions did you have to placing the stamps in one of several categories rather than in contrasting pairs? Make your comments from memory or by listening to a few minutes of the audio recordings you made of the conversations during the separate groupings in each activity.

_____
_____
_____
_____
_____
_____

Here are some differences other people have noted:

> Putting stamps in columns was a lot easier than juxtaposing them into contrasting pairs.

> When I sorted the stamps with my hands I tried to put more stamps in each column than when I simply looked at the stamps; in fact, I took each stamp and placed it under each column or "lens" to see whether there was, say, wood in it.

> I felt that if I made a mistake in sorting the stamps with my fingers it did not matter; I simply had to move the stamp to another place. Writing the numbers based on just looking at the stamps made me more tentative.

> I often pulled stamps out of the hands of my partner because I wanted to try a different grouping and I needed to actually put the stamp in the column.

> As I sorted the stamps themselves, I heard myself saying "this goes there; this one does, too" over and over again.

Many people who grouped the stamps found it useful to move the pictures of the stamps around, placing them in the separate columns; this may provide a suggestion for thinking about lessons. Try grouping excerpts from lessons in the same way. Later in this book you will be asked to group excerpts from classes into columns using only your visual sense. If you prefer to use both your visual and tactile sense, feel free to copy each excerpt in lists on a separate note card. Then you can move the cards around under various column headings rather than simply visually "moving" the excerpts

YOUR PERCEPTION OF THE WORLD

The process of grouping is central to many who write about education. Frank Smith, who has written widely about the reading process, provides one description of the process of grouping—matching titles, columns, or labels with examples—that you have been engaged in:

> To categorize means to treat some objects or events as the same yet as different from other objects or events.... No living organism could survive if it treated everything in its experience as the same.... But similarly, no living organism could survive if it treated everything in its experience as different.... The categories that we all observe, which are part of our theories of the world, are visually quite arbitrary.... The category system that is part of our theory of the world in our heads is essential for making sense of the world. Anything we do that we cannot relate to a category will not make sense; we shall be bewildered. Our categories, in other words, are the basis of our perception of the world.
>
> (Smith, 1971, pp. 59, 60)

The idea that the grouping we all do every day is the "basis of our perception of the world" is considered helpful in learning to read. Thus, if we see a newspaper headline about hiking, when we come across the word *cardinal*, we can predict it will be the name of a bird. Under a headline on church matters with the dateline Vatican City, if we see the word *cardinal*, we would attribute the meaning of religious title to the word and think of men, not birds. In the sports section, *Cardinals* would evoke in many the name of a team.

On the other hand, a person's "perception of the world" can be a hindrance. If we associate people in charge with men who wear suits, shirts, and ties, we may, upon entering an office with a woman in a dress in it, ask "Where is the manager?" when in fact the person in front of us is the manager. Seeing the word *eggplant* on a menu, a person unfamiliar with the vegetable once said, "I don"t think I'll order that because I don't like eggs." English-speaking people who see "hôtel de ville" above many ornate buildings in small towns in France are sometimes disappointed to find that the rooms they sought to book in the "hotel" are in fact offices for city hall bureaucrats.

Activity 5

In the spaces below, consider how your perception of the world helped or hindered your grouping of stamps. For example, some say that they cannot sort pictures of items that they have no background on. Without knowing who Freeman or Pocahontas was, they cannot even consider grouping them. Others say the opposite: Since there are no right answers, they can ignore the actual facts of who the people were and simply try to see details in the pictures that do not depend on historical knowledge but on what one sees.

Others who feel it is important to do an activity in sequence find it easy to sort the stamps by finding a feature in stamp #1 and then look for the same feature in each stamp in sequence. Of course, after seeing other labels, they realize that this systematic sequencing prevents them from seeing any feature in stamps #2 through #13 that does not occur in the first stamp. One sorter, associating grouping with the grouping of shapes he had recently observed in a nursery school, could think of nothing but shapes in his grouping. Thus, he saw not only the globes in stamps #2, #3, and #7 but the circles around the postage rate in stamps #2, #3, #7, #10, #12, and #13. Even the letter *o* in postage, expedition, and so forth was seen only as a circle, to say nothing of the discus in the hand of the athlete in #7 and the frame around Columbus in #4.

How your "theory of the world"—labels, preconceived notions, perceptions, lenses—contributed to grouping the stamps

_____
_____
_____
_____
_____
_____
_____
_____

How your "theory of the world"—labels, preconceived notions, perceptions, lenses—hindered grouping the stamps

_____
_____
_____
_____
_____
_____
_____
_____

Looking at the comments of those who did these activities before you, I have noticed that many think that their "theory of the world" hindered their grouping because they tended to see only features such as the postage rate and large objects pictured in the foreground. Many noticed words on the stamps ("Pocahontas" on #9 is easily picked up). But they said the words sometimes drew their attention away from other visual items such as the shields on the same stamp, which though similar in size to the letters and numbers, were not part of their usual theories of the world. Smith's quote on the reading process reminds us that perceptions of the world stem from categories that "are quite arbitrary."

Other people point out that once they focused on one patriotic symbol, other symbols were "filtered" out. Also, the fact that we expect to see *U.S.* on American stamps and the fact that some rendition of *U.S.* is printed on all the stamps except one hindered some from noticing that the 5-cent Pilgrim Tercentary (#13) in fact has no explicit indication that it is a stamp from the United States. Analysis of individual perception deserves our closer attention.

BECOMING AWARE OF THE EFFECT OF FILTERS

The need to fit the world into the category system we already have so that we can make sense of it often prevents us from seeing reality that does not fit into our system. Bateson, a noted thinker in ecology and many other fields, describes this phenomenon:

> ... the obvious can be very difficult for people to see. That is because people are self-corrective systems. They are self-corrective against disturbance, and if the obvious is not of a kind that they can easily assimilate without internal disturbance, their self-corrective mechanisms work to sidetrack it, to hide it, even to the extent of shutting off various parts of the process of perception. Disturbing information can be framed like a pearl so that it doesn't make a nuisance of itself; and this will be done, according to the understanding of the system itself of what would be a nuisance. This too—the premise regarding what would cause disturbance—is something which is learned and then becomes perpetuated or conserved.
>
> (Bateson, 1972, p. 429)

In observing classes, the same phenomenon occurs. If we think rapport is important, we will group what we see into the categories *rapport/ no rapport*. If we think enthusiasm is important, we will look for evidence of enthusiasm. Looking at different classes with the same perceptions or filters  we have been using for a long time is unlikely to reveal anything not previously seen, just as looking at stamps without the command to fit them into categories that are not naturally part of our perception or belief system may prevent us from seeing features of stamps that do not match our categories.

BUILDING PERCEPTIONS

When we began to look for features in Activity 1 in order to establish a category or group, each item we noticed in one stamp became a category that we could look for in the other stamps. One perception was built upon another.

Alone we are often bewildered. We can only come up with features that are important in *our* perception of the world. With a partner we are able to begin to consider another view if our partner gives us a category we do not have. And in Activity 2, categories were provided that a number of different individuals had made. Individual perception can be modified either by using someone else's label or lens, or by using our own labels in a new way.

A Two-step Process

In looking at stamps or at teaching, we each have beliefs about what is significant. If we look only for what we consider significant, we are likely to miss a lot. To see something that is not part of our theory of the world—our belief system—either in a stamp or a class, two steps are necessary.

In step 1, we need to put down a word describing a feature we saw in the stamp or in the teaching act that is based on our perception—the title for one column. Then, we have to put down a word describing an opposite feature but one related to the first—a contrasting title. For example water might be the first feature we noticed looking at the 10-cent Lindbergh (#1). To find other stamps with and without water forces us to look at scenes on stamps that on first looking seem totally dry, such as the 5-cent signing of the compact aboard the *Mayflower* (#13).

A column heading for classroom talk might be *Questions to which the teacher knew the answer*. Just as *those without water* is juxtaposed to *those with water* in grouping stamps, so we can juxtapose *Questions the teacher did not know the answer to* with *Questions to which the teacher knew the answer*.

After we establish the groupings—the lenses we are going to use—we have to match examples that fit the categories we establish.

In step 2, we need to get a word describing a feature we did not notice from some other source, such as a colleague. Once we have labels, categories, or lenses from others, we simply have to follow the same steps we take with our own features.

In engaging in this process, it is critical to remember that agreement is not the goal. Seeing something we have not seen before is the goal. Once we provide a name of a category, which is a representation of our theory of the world, we have to discuss which items fit the category. Such a discussion requires some disagreement and some questions about both the meaning of the category and the items that fit the category. We have to match, rematch, and match again the words we use to refer to reality and samples of the reality itself. After the disagreements and uncertainty comes understanding and the different kind of certainty discussed in the introduction to this book.

Using Sampling

When grouping stamps, the reality consists of the stamps. In the case of teaching, part of the reality consists of recordings, transcripts, snapshots, or drawings of some classroom events or exercises from textbooks, tests, or syllabuses. In both cases, the amount of reality we are exploring is small, based on two premises: one, a small amount of data can provide a great amount of information*, and two, seeing multiple features of a small sample of reality in precise detail will make it easier to change what we do.

For example, if we observe a teacher saying "very good" after a student response at the beginning of a question/answer segment of a class, nine times out of ten the teacher will say "very good" during the entire segment. During the same segment, if the teacher starts to call students by name less than a second after the question is uttered, it is likely the same amount of time will be allowed throughout the segment. Looking at three or four instances of "very good" and the amount of times provided for students to consider their responses will thus likely reveal the same pattern as looking at thirty or forty instances of the same practices. Even

---

*Of course, larger bits of communication can be examined specifically as well. One can analyze types of activities as well as types of single communications. The way of looking is what is central. The belief that whatever we analyze is patterned means that the size of the data we are exploring can vary.

though it is worthwhile to see whether a pattern of practices holds for an entire segment once in a while, the idea of sampling is no different from the idea behind medical tests that use samples of blood to check the entire organ or the samples behind public opinion polling.

By looking at the three or four instances of "very good" over and over, rather than looking at forty once, we might more likely notice features such as these: (1) The teacher begins to say "very good" before the student completes the response, thus suggesting the words might not function purely as a positive comment, since at the time it is being said it is not clear whether the response will be correct or not; (2) students sometimes continue their response after "very good" has been said, suggesting that they do not hear the words; (3) as the teacher says "very good," the teacher's eyes are usually focused on the student about to be called on rather than the student who has just responded, thus suggesting the words may function partly as a transition signal for both the teacher and students.

By identifying a specific practice such as the use of "very good" to play with rather than a general topic such as *feedback*, alternative practices can more practically be substituted and subsequently analyzed. We might write three choices on the blackboard; for example: (1) "100% correct," (2) "on the right track," (3) "incorrect." After each student response, the teacher could note in the lesson plan that one of the three choices was to be pointed to after a student response.

Some people starve themselves for a few days when dieting and then go back to their previous patterns of eating. Other dieters decrease the  amount of butter they use slightly one week. Then the next week they also decrease the amount of sugar they use. During the third week of their diet, they stop putting raisins on their cereal. In addition, each week for about 6 weeks, they add 4 minutes to their daily walk. Over time, each small change can be easily monitored and is often more likely to lead to long-term changes in weight than sudden, crash diets will.

Activity 6

Vygotsky, the noted Russian psychologist, saw thinking as *connecting*: "Every thought tends to connect something with something else, to establish a relationship between things" (1962, p. 125). This activity asks you to look at places in your conversations with your partner where you were in the process of building interpretations. Either try to recall some of your comments during your stamp-grouping conversations or listen to a few minutes of the tape you made. Note, in the spaces below, agreements and disagreements you felt with someone else's perceptions. Then consider how both agreements and disagreements led to and blocked connections.

Some agreements
_____
_____
_____

The Grouping Process ■ 23

_____

Some disagreements

_____

RECOGNIZING JUDGMENT

Activity 7

During any of the groupings, can you remember any judgments about the stamps you or your partner made? Other than using words such as *ugly* or *beautiful* as categories for grouping, did either of you group the stamps with labels such as *crazy-looking stamp, boring stamp, poorly printed stamp*? In the space below, write any judgments you recall or that you pick up from the tape.

_____

Many partners find it hard to recall any judgments of the stamps at all. Some recall judgments about the activity itself, though: "What a silly thing to do," "How time-consuming," or "Childish but interesting." Some recall saying they liked some stamps or disliked others but don't feel they made any judgments. The directions to put the stamps in a number of contrasting pairs and to match titles with individual stamps might have decreased the frequency of judgments used to attribute value to the stamps. But I have found that the number of judgments made about stamps is strikingly small in comparison with the number found in a tape of similar length in which two people are having conversations about teaching practices.

Does familiarity breed judgment? A tape recording of a conversation between two stamp dealers discussing the actual stamps (in color, of course) would have just as many judgments as many conversations about beliefs and teaching practices between a supervisor and teacher or between two teachers. Stamp dealers normally do not group stamps into those with water in them or not, but they do group them on the basis of technical features, such as the number of perforations in each 2 centimeters, or the types of watermarks in the paper, or the type of printing process used. Mainly, stamp dealers say things like "extremely fine centering"—referring to the amount of white selvage on each side of the frame. Even the technical features are ultimately used to support the evaluation of a particular stamp, not to describe it for its own sake.

Below are some excerpts from an auction catalog to capture the types of judgments some stamp dealers make. These comments were made about the stamps we have worked with, although they are about other copies of them. If you underline any and all words you think are *not* judgments, the preponderance of judgments will be even more striking than it seems from a quick reading of the comments.

> 1-cent Columbian (#4): marvelously well centered; huge margins; pristine radiance; sumptuous color
>
> 5-cent Trans-Mississippi (#8): a fabulously fresh stamp which possesses magnificent, eye-arresting color, a razor-sharp impression, mathematical centering, brilliantly fresh
>
> $5 Carmine and blue (#10): a gorgeous single; flawlessly centered amid extravagantly large margins; lovely rich colors, extremely fine; a gem; premium example
>
> 24-cent Carmine rose and blue (#12): an eye-arresting jumbo-margined mint example; perfectly centered amid enormously large margins; luxuriant colors; crisp and uniformly even perforations all around add to this stamp's sensational appearance; superb
>
> $2.60 Blue (#3): fabulously well centered; sensational impression; sumptuous color; exceptional in every respect, flawless; the most exciting copy we have had the pleasure to offer

I was able to underline only twenty words, including function words such as *a* out of the 100 or so in the excerpts. If the aim is to determine worth, we will obviously judge to evaluate, whatever we are looking at. Though some of the judgments we make while visiting classes are seemingly negative—"You call yourself a teacher? I'll show you how to teach!"—rather than positive—the comments from the stamp auction catalog—the judgments are almost as frequent as those made by stamp dealers.

It seems that the judgments we make are determined by our intentions. Whether the discussion is about stamps or lessons and textbooks, if our aim is to evaluate, the conversation will be packed with judgments that reflect our preconceived notions and beliefs about what we value.

If we want to have conversations in which we explore, rather than judge, in which we try to see something we have not seen before rather than to find evidence to support the beliefs and notions we already have, then we need to have contrasting conversations. We need to engage in activities that somehow enable us to use our judgments to explore rather

 than to evaluate and to move beyond our present preconceived notions and beliefs and use different theories, or lenses, to see the world.

*W*HAT HAVE WE LEARNED ABOUT LOOKING?

Take a moment and think about one or two lessons you learned or an insight you gained about observing lessons from the activities in this section. If you like, write down your thoughts as an additional optional activity on these lines.

___

___

___

___

___

___

___

Conclusions that others have made from their explorations up to this point include:

Our perceptions can limit what we see.

Multiple analyses of small amounts of data can reveal a great deal; even data that we think have only two or three features often have many, many more.

Multiple interpretations of what is seen are not only possible, but vital for understanding.

Though some of these conclusions might seem obvious, they are often overlooked, and, even when noticed, are not often applied to the exploration of our beliefs and teaching practices.

Grouping the stamps illustrates one meaning of English poet William Blake's "To see a World in a Grain of Sand/And a Heaven in a Wild Flower" ("Auguries of Innocence," 1863), since, as we keep looking, we see more and more. Though Blake's lines may imply we each see the same world, his engravings remind us that each of us has a very different view of the world in each grain of sand.

I hope that the multiple characteristics of the stamps reminds you of the multiple characteristics of each communication in teaching. And, when we dwell on any one characteristic, we fail to see other ones. Looking at the postage rate is important for getting the mail through, but while focusing on the rate we fail to see the figure, the caption, the design, or the date.

Looking at the teacher when we observe a class can be important for seeing some moves we might make in the role of teacher. But with our eyes on the teacher, we fail to see the students. With our ears listening to what is said, we fail to see communications made with the participants' bodies. While sketching body language, we tune out what is being said. The usual statements, such as "The teacher was enthusiastic, so the students were involved" symbolizes the fact that we often note single characteristics of phenomena rather than multiple characteristics. It also indicates our tendency to explain an effect such as student involvement with one cause such as teacher enthusiasm, rather than with multiple causes: teacher enthusiasm, plus emphasis on dates and names, plus careful listening to student responses exhibited by comments such as "date is close but not exact," plus periods of teacher silence to allow students to teach so that students can explore a range of evaluations from people who ask them questions. And, of course, as pointed out earlier, it also indicates the significance we have attached to enthusiasm.

The grouping activities illustrated the fact that the theories of the world that allow us to cope with reality also trap us——"Looking at the postage rate is important for getting the mail through, but while focusing on the rate we fail to see the figure or the caption or the design or the date." In the next section, you will try grouping some actual communications from classes, textbooks, or tests in the same way that you grouped the stamps. This will "bring home" the previous explanations and prepare you to explore a variety of classroom applications in Part Two.

RECONSTRUCTING OBSERVED LESSONS

When I started to observe classes, I made many mental notes during the lesson. Then in the discussion after, I often jotted down some memories of the lesson. I took no pencil-and-paper notes during the lesson. When I observe classes with people who are observing for the first few times, I find that my original practice seems to be the rule with them. We seem to treat lessons we observe the same way we treat other events in life: We simply observe them.

A detective on the long-popular American television series "Dragnet" started his interviews of witnesses to crimes with a line that became famous: "All I want is the facts." Though the detective took notes as he interviewed these witnesses, I never saw the witnesses produce notes of what they had observed at the scenes of the crimes. When in daily life do we write down precise observations? Who takes notes while watching TV, for example? So, why would we take notes when we observe a class live or a video of a class?

RECORDING OBSERVATIONS

Activity 8

The person who wrote the notes below had been instructed to take notes while observing a class. The resulting material contains some "facts" and some other types of communications. With another teacher, decide which lines you consider facts and which are something else. Write an *f* for fact on the broken lines next to the communications you consider facts. (Ignore the long, unbroken lines for now.) Again: There are no wrong answers!

1. Teacher said, "What are you holding?" ___ _____
2. One student repeated, "What you hold?" ___ _____
3. Teacher shook head sideways. ___ _____
4. Teacher repeated, "What are you holding?" ___ _____
5. Teacher emphasized *are* and *ing* when saying, "What are you holding?" ___ _____
6. He said the words too quickly. ___ _____
7. He used a rapid rate. ___ _____
8. He offset the speed with repeated models. ___ _____
9. Some students were not participating. ___ _____
10. It appeared that one or two students were catching the pattern. ___ _____
11. The lesson was very clear. ___ _____

28 ■ Learning to Look

12. He used the blackboard for writing the model he had said orally.
    --- _____

13. He held up two fingers when he wanted a two-word answer.
    --- _____

Thinking about the Alternatives

Compare which items you and your partner wrote an *f* next to with those of other partners. The process you have to engage in in order to see what you and your partner each mean by the word *fact* is more important than seeing what I mean by the word. My labeling is neither correct nor incorrect but simply reveals how I use the word *fact*.

I put an *f* next to 1 through 5, 12, and 13. I believe, for example, that "rapid rate" in line 7 is not a fact because it is more interpretative and less descriptive than "repeated" in line 4. I further believe that "too quickly" in line 6 is more judgmental than "a rapid rate" in line 7. Police stop us for speeding, after all, not for going at a rapid rate. However, I can see that "repeated" in line 4 is more interpretative than "said" in line 1 because "repeated" implies that the teacher rendered the line the same way as in line 1, without changing the intonation or tone of voice.

Now go back to the unbroken lines next to an item you did not label as fact and, without your partner, write out words on the blank lines that you think characterize or describe those items. For example, if item 6 is not fact in your view, you may, as I did, write *interpretation* there.

I consider item 8 to be an explanation. The observer seems to be trying to give a reason for the rapid rate he used. I might use the word *justification* for the same reason.

The statement in item 9, "Some students were not participating," would seem one that could be verified, indicating a fact. But calling this a fact implies that we all have the same understanding of *participating*. Does *participating* mean paying attention, following, speaking, listening, volunteering to respond, or something else? Since *participation* has multiple meanings for me, I call line 9 an *interpretation*. *Judgment* is a word I'd also consider here, since the statement implies that all the students, not just some students should be participating.

Saying a lesson is "clear," as in 11, is a judgment to me, just as is terrible or terrific, guilty or innocent, marvelously well centered, or fabulously fresh.

While there is no reason that you, your partner, and I should agree on the descriptors, or words we use to characterize individual lines, it is vital that we see that the descriptor or label we use fits the meaning we attribute to a specific line.

Activity 9

Now apply your grouping skills to the teaching excerpt from Activity 8. What are the other words or descriptors we can apply to characterize, label, or group the lines that were written by an observer during a lesson? The chart on the next page lists some possibilities.

You or the teacher you work with should enter the lines written by the observer where they seem to fit. For example, I'd write "What are you holding?" in lines 1 and 4 under "transcription." And, I'd write "teacher said" in line 1 under "narration."

transcription	narration	something else

Thinking about the Alternatives

The words in quotation marks in lines 1, 2, and 4 qualify as transcription, if *transcription* means writing words that are heard. If the word means writing down the phonetic spelling of utterances, then none of the lines qualify. Nor do any lines qualify if *transcription* means writing down only words that are heard, without any description of how they were said or who said them. If the word means writing down what was said or done by the participants, we have to add line 12 to the column marked *transcription*, since holding up two fingers is obviously something someone did.

Narration might be easier. Unfortunately, or rather, naturally, *narration* also can mean more than one thing. If you were asked to play the part of a narrator, you would have to say "Teacher said" when reading line 1. An actor or actress could then say the rest of the line "Where are you going?" Using this meaning, lines 1, 2, 4, and 5 contain both narrative material and transcribed material.

Since many fiction authors present the type of, what I consider to be, interpretative comments in their stories, items 6 to 13 could easily be considered narration also. They tell a kind of story. But they seem different from the words before the quotation marks, which would be read by a narrator in items 1, 2, 4, and 5. "Said," "repeated," or "emphasized" seem different from "offset" or "clear." But perhaps the difference is not sufficient to call them "something else." We would have to limit *narration* to mean what a person says before the words in quotation marks if we wanted to put lines 6 to 13 under *something else*.

Distinguishing between *transcription*, *narration*, and *something else* might be easier than determining exactly what *transcription* means when we have an audio recording before us and a pencil in hand, poised above a blank pad. Should we just write down the words that are said? Should we ignore the pauses, the "uhs" and "ohs," and the tone of voice used? Should we show variations in pronunciation by using phonetic script?

How do we show when two speakers are saying words at the same time? Should we write the lines like the lines in a play, one after the other? Or should we write all the words one speaker says in one column, the other speaker's utterances in a second? Then we could see the words of each speaker lined up, like this:

JOHN: Where's the milk?
JOANNE: In the fridge.
JOHN: I don't see it.
JOANNE: Behind the juice, top shelf.

From a video recording more data are available—and so there are more questions. Should we add some notes to show the position of people, objects that are pointed to? Should we describe facial expressions such as a smile, or gestures such as the shaking of a head sideways?

In fact, whether we respond "Yes" or "No" to all of the above questions, we have to realize that *any* transcription we make is partial. Any transcription, like any narration, whether made during an observation or afterwards, involves selection.

Which is better: a narration, a transcription, a recording, or a recollection? That question is not consistent with the theme of this book. What we need to concentrate on are the differences between the types of collected data. Take, for example, the quote in the introduction: "You call yourself a teacher? I'll show you how to teach!" You have only my recollection of what the supervisor said. I collected only one type of data. If I had a video recording of the scene, we might be able to determine if the teacher's intonation was ironic, humorous, sarcastic, supportive, or matter-of-fact. If I had a text written by this particular teacher, to describe his ideas about teaching and observations, I could compare his ideas with the words I heard. Knowing that different data show different realities at least allows us to generate a range of interpretations. Now we will see what happens when we supplement one kind of observation recording with another.

Activity 10

Below I have made some additions to the notes we read in Activity 8, after looking at a video recording of the lesson. The additions are shown in brackets.

Put an *f* for fact on the broken line next to those groups of words in brackets that you consider facts.

1. Teacher said, "What are you holding?" [student addressed was holding a beret; teacher was looking at student] ___

2. One student repeated, "What you hold?" [student said words with rising intonation and moved left hand up to left chin as if he was puzzled; did not look at the beret he was holding] ___

3. Teacher shook head sideways. [as he shook his head sideways, the student was looking at the beret in his hands—did not seem to notice the shaking of the teacher's head] ___

4. Teacher repeated, "What are you holding?" [teacher moved closer to the student as he repeated the words and pointed to the beret on the student's lap] ___

5. Teacher emphasized *are* and *ing* when saying, "What are you holding?" [teacher looked at the student as if to say, "Why can't you say the words right?"] ___

6. He said the words too quickly. [nodded his head up and down as he said the words] ___

7. He used a rapid rate. [moved his hands as he said the words] ___

8. He offset the speed with repeated models. [hearing the words over and over made them sound a bit like gibberish] ___

9. Some students were not participating. [Romero was looking at his hands, not the student speaking] ___

10. It appeared that one or two students were catching the pattern. [hard to see any way to show students catching the pattern since only one student was saying words at this point] ___

11. The lesson was very clear. [not sure what the point was—seemed to be the *to be* plus *ing* form] ___

12. He used the blackboard for writing the model he had said orally. [students did not look at the blackboard] ___

13. He held up two fingers when he wanted a two-word answer. [he also wrote on the board "a beret" and "I'm holding a beret," to contrast the long and short responses] ___

Thinking about the Alternatives

The process of arguing about the meaning you and your partner each attach to the word *fact* is the critical step here. My comments, below, reflect my understanding of the meanings of the words—not the right answers. Matching items or examples with the words we use as labels enables each of us to see more clearly the meaning we each attribute to those labels or descriptors.

I put an *f* next to the bracketed words with items 1, 4, 6, 7, 9, and 12. In item 2, the single word "puzzled" prevented me from considering the more than twenty-five other words as facts. If "as if he was puzzled" were removed, I would have been able to write an *f* next to the words there. In item 3, the words "did not seem to notice" changed *fact* to interpretation for me because whether the person did or did not notice is different from "looking at his hands." In item 5 "as if to say" would not be accepted by the detective in "Dragnet," nor perhaps by many judges, either. The use of "too quickly" in 6 sounds like a law enforcement officer talking to a delinquent driver rather than a car enthusiast talking about the speed of automobiles, but the words in brackets seem neutral. In 8, we have a judgment signaled by "gibberish." Item 10 is a type of explanation of why the original interpretation ("it appeared that one or two students were catching the pattern") cannot be supported. And 13 is an explanation of why the teacher did what he did—like attributing a motive to a criminal—and is more than a fact.

Just as a person trying to sell stamps will make positive judgments—"fantastic centering"—while the person buying will make negative judgments—"faded color"—so our judgments about classes can be positive or negative and tend to reflect the roles we are in and our own beliefs rather than the value of what we are observing.

Optional Activity: Using Facts

In the appendix of supplemental activities you will find Activity 10A. It provides practice in assigning each of the thirteen items we have been working with to the categories *transcription or narrative details to describe, transcriptions or narrative details used to support judgments and interpretations,* or those that do neither *(neutral).*

Activity 11

In the by-now-familiar thirteen lines, reprinted below, write a plus sign (+) on the broken lines next to those items you think make the teacher look good and a minus sign (−) next to the lines you think make the teacher look bad.

1. Teacher said, "What are you holding?" [student addressed was holding a beret; teacher was looking at student] ___

2. One student repeated, "What you hold?" [student said words with rising intonation and moved left hand up to left chin as if he was puzzled; did not look at the beret he was holding] ___

3. Teacher shook head sideways. [as he shook his head sideways, the student was looking at the beret in his hands—did not seem to notice the shaking of the teacher's head] ___

4. Teacher repeated, "What are you holding?" [teacher moved closer to the student as he repeated the words and pointed to the beret on the student's lap] ___

5. Teacher emphasized *are* and *ing* when saying, "What are you holding?" [teacher looked at the student as if to say, "Why can't you say the words right?"] ___

6. He said the words too quickly. [nodded his head up and down as he said the words] ___

7. He used a rapid rate. [moved his hands as he said the words] ___

8. He offset the speed with repeated models. [hearing the words over and over made them sound a bit like gibberish] ___

9. Some students were not participating. [Romero was looking at his hands, not the student speaking] ___

10. It appeared that one or two students were catching the pattern. [hard to see any way to show students catching the pattern since only one student was saying words at this point] ___

11. The lesson was very clear. [not sure what the point was—seemed to be the *to be* plus *ing* form] ___

12. He used the blackboard for writing the model he had said orally. [students did not look at the blackboard] ___

13. He held up two fingers when he wanted a two-word answer. [he also wrote on the board "a beret" and "I'm holding a beret," to contrast the long and short responses] ___

It is possible to argue that each line can be either positive or negative depending on the beliefs we each have and the goals we have set for teaching or observing. For example, if you as a teacher think people concentrate more when the task is harder and you think that speaking quickly is more difficult, then you will write a plus sign next to 6, "He said the words too quickly," and 7, "He used a rapid rate." If you think that speaking quickly to a non-native speaker of a language is confusing and makes it harder to follow, you will write a minus sign.

Thinking about the Alternatives

The only explanation I thought made the teacher look good was in item 13, "to contrast the long and short responses." "Puzzled" in 2, "did not seem to notice" in 3, "as if to say 'Why can't you say the words right?' " in 5, "gibberish" in 8, "hard to see" in 10, and "not sure what the point was" in 11 all have negative connotations to me. Jack Webb from "Dragnet" would have been dismayed with the "facts" that were selected to "convict" the teacher, even if he had thought the teacher was guilty.

While we often have a clear idea of what we consider positive or negative, just as often we probably forget that one person's positive can be another person's negative. And often we forget that what we attribute to the words, or any other phenomena we are judging does not mean that the phenomena themselves are good or bad. As a tennis coach who advocates suspending judgments to more clearly see tennis shots wrote, "Judgments are our personal, ego reactions to the sights, sounds, feelings and thoughts within our experience" (Gallwey, 1974, p. 34). Or, to paraphrase one of Shakespeare's characters, "things are neither good nor bad but thinking makes them so."

We must remember that our experience and someone else's are usually different. By trying to see how what we mark with a minus can be positive and how what we mark with a plus sign can be negative, we can attempt to see another's experience. Thus, if we believe that group work is vital to teaching, it can be instructive to pretend to be a supervisor who considers group work disruptive. By looking at the possibility that the disruptive nature of group work might interfere with learning, we might be able to generate some practices that decrease the noise during group work.

Activity 12

I have selected some of the lines from the thirteen items we have been looking at for this activity. Even though you have not seen the tape of the lesson on which the notes were taken, with your partner try to rewrite a few of the lines added in brackets.

Cross out those words you and your partner think have a negative connotation. Substitute words that have a positive connotation and rewrite the comments on the blank lines preceded with plus signs. For example, in item 2, if you think "puzzled" has a negative connotation, you might cross it out and substitute "fascinated" and rewrite "as if he was fascinated."

Substitute words with a negative connotation for those with a positive connotation and rewrite the comments next to the minus sign. For example, if "offset the speed with repeated models" in 8 seems favorable to you, you would cross out "offset" and write something such as "failed to compensate for the speed with repeated models." When you have finished, compare your comments with those written by others.

2. One student repeated, "What you hold?" [student said words with rising intonation and moved left hand up to left chin as if he was puzzled; did not look at the beret he was holding]

+ _____
_____
_____
_____

− _____
_____
_____
_____

5. Teacher emphasized *are* and *ing* when saying, "What are you holding?" [teacher looked at the student as if to say, "Why can't you say the words right?"]

+ _____
_____
_____
_____

− _____
_____
_____
_____

7. He used a rapid rate. [moved his hands as he said the words]

+ _____
_____
_____
_____

− _____
_____
_____
_____

Reconstructing Observed Lessons

8. He offset the speed with repeated models. [hearing the words over and over made them sound a bit like gibberish]

\+ _____

\- _____

13. He held up two fingers when he wanted a two-word answer. [he also wrote on the board "a beret" and "I'm holding a beret," to contrast the long and short responses]

\+ _____

\- _____

Thinking about the Alternatives

For "puzzled" in item 2, one observer substituted "very curious" and another "pensive," arguing that moving one's hand to one's chin to support the head is similar to the position of the hand in Rodin's sculpture *The Thinker*—to many a symbol of thought, concentration, and curiosity.

In item 5, why could the teacher's look not mean "You can say the words right, it's easy"? The "rapid rate" in 7 could be called "normal," "natural," or "at the rate a native speaker would say it," interpretations that sound either neutral or even positive.

In 8, "He complemented the speed" sounds more positive than "he offset the speed" to some. Rather than saying something sounded like "gibberish," it could be said "hearing the words over and over showed that the teacher was keen on having the students hear the form and the sounds rather than attending to the meaning."

Some see the reason given in 13 for the teacher writing two patterns on the board as positive: "to contrast the long and short responses." Those who do have rewritten the reason in ways to imply a negative reason: "written words can only interfere with oral language" or "showing two different answers confuses the students since they don't know whether the

36 ■ Learning to Look

teacher holding up two fingers is telling them to give two answers or one answer with two words in it; the signals are ambiguous."

There are obviously other possible positive interpretations of both these and other words you might consider negative. These are simply examples.

We can use any one of the positive or negative judgments as a starting point to consider alternatives. For example, "rapid rate" in 7 opens up the area of rate of delivery for exploration. Whether we think the models have been given very slow, slow, fast, very fast, normally, or any place in between, we can alter the speed in subsequent lessons and, over time, we can alter speed within the same lesson. The judgments evoked by the range of meanings of the teacher's signal in line 13, "He held up two fingers," can serve as a stimulus to explore the meanings students attribute to signals.

In subsequent lessons, we could use a series of hand signals. First we could ask students to draw the signals. Then, we could ask students to write down what message the students thought each signal was sending. The sketches might show us that what we considered the signal—holding up two fingers—was missed by the students. Some might draw the position of our head or the expression on our face rather than the position of our fingers. Those who consider the fingers the signal might write a range of meanings that are different from the ones we intended. We can use each judgment we and others make as a source for generating alternatives rather than as an order to stop a particular practice or increase the use of another practice. Judgments can be sources of exploration rather than of evaluation.

SEEKING DIFFERENT REPRESENTATIONS OF REALITY

There are of course many perspectives that could be brought to bear on the lesson "What are you holding," which we have viewed in the past few activities. As you know from your work grouping stamps, one way to present other views of reality is to develop titles for types/groups of communications that you want to extract from the data. Here are a few possibilities:

value-free	with values
without feelings	with feelings
what happened	what happened plus
words alone	words plus extras from the voice box and mouth
words alone	words plus body language
what happened	what happened related to goals
transcription deals with position or location of participants	transcription does not deal with the location or position of participants
important facts	unimportant facts
details	general points
facts to prove that the lesson is boring	facts to prove that the lesson is engaging
practices that deal with form	practices that deal with meaning

Activity 13

Select one of the above pairs of groupings, write it in the blank line after "Your selection." Then, on the bracketed blank lines below each of the thirteen observations add words to embellish the original observations so that you have new notes that fit your selection of grouping titles. When you have finished, compare what you did with what others did.

> Your selection: _____
>
> 1. Teacher said, "What are you holding?"
>   [_____]
> 2. One student repeated, "What you hold?"
>   [_____]
> 3. Teacher shook head sideways.
>   [_____]
> 4. Teacher repeated, "What are you holding?"
>   [_____]
> 5. Teacher emphasized *are* and *ing* when saying, "What are you holding?"
>   [_____]
> 6. He said the words too quickly.
>   [_____]
> 7. He used a rapid rate.
>   [_____]
> 8. He offset the speed with repeated models.
>   [_____]
> 9. Some students were not participating.
>   [_____]
> 10. It appeared that one or two students were catching the pattern.
>   [_____]
> 11. The lesson was very clear.
>   [_____]
> 12. He used the blackboard for writing the model he had said orally.
>   [_____]
> 13. He held up two fingers when he wanted a two-word answer.
>   [_____]

Thinking about the Alternatives

Using the pair of titles *what happened/what happened related to goals* to group the observations, the first step one teacher took during this conversation was to state a goal. The goal stated was "provide samples of a language for students to hear and associate an action with the model." Given this goal, lines 1 and 4 are congruent with the goal since the model is given in these lines. Line 8 suggests that other models were spoken as well. The communications after the student said the model incorrectly are not in line with the goal since they involve production rather than simply hearing. It is not clear from the transcript of line 1 that the holding of the beret (as embellished from Activity 10) is an action that is supposed to be associated with the model. Writing the model on the board, reported in line 12, does not appeal to the students' ears, but their eyes. The same can be said for the two fingers in line 13.

Here are words added to embellish the lines to meet the title *what happened related to goals*:

1. Because the goal was to provide the model as much as possible, teacher said: "What are you holding?"

2. One student repeated "What you hold?" and because there is an error, the goal of providing the model as much as possible is not met.

3. Teacher shook head sideways is an unfortunate behavior since it in no way provides the model; the student has no way to know where the error is since no model is given.

The two teachers who selected the titles *form/meaning*, found that all the observations as written seemed to deal only with form. Consequently, they found they had to write the same type of embellishments for each observation. Here are some of their embellishments:

1. Teacher said "What are you holding?" so that the students could recognize the sounds sequence of words in the pattern.

2. One student repeated "What you hold?" showing that the form of the present participle and the use of the verb to be has not been recognized or remembered.

3. Teacher shook head sideways. In order to stress to the student the importance of the correct form, the teacher indicated that the student's rendition of the pattern was incorrect when the student said "What you hold?"

HOW WE SELECT AFFECTS WHAT WE SELECT

The activities in this section were designed to get you to realize that there are many different ways of collecting and grouping data. For example, in research in which you have only one chance to see the data you are analyzing, you do not have the benefits that a tape or videotape recorder provides. Here is how one scholar lamented the usual lot of researchers:

The explorer returns after a long absence with bottles, boxes and bags. On arrival he exclaims, in a variety of modest phrases, "Look what I've found!," but it takes him longer to sort out his findings than it did to collect them. . . . The more he analyses his material the more he feels that if only he could make the journey again in the light of the knowledge he now has his miscellaneous collection could be made more orderly, coherent and complete.

(Michaels, 1987, p. 2)

With recordings, in fact, you can make "the journey again in the light of the knowledge" you have. You and your partner can write notes from small segments of lessons you observe live. And then, after some grouping of the communications you wrote, you can rewind and listen again to audio- and videotapes to make different notes and different types of transcriptions. You can watch videotapes at fast speed, regular speed, frame by frame, and backwards, with or without the sound.

But the point of this section is not just to emphasize the potential value of taping classes nor even of taking notes when you observe live. Rather the purpose of the grouping activities, the purpose of substituting words with negative connotations for words with positive connotations, or vice versa, has been to make us conscious—each time we observe, transcribe tapes, or view lessons on video—of *how* we are selecting.

What I hope you will gain from this book is the realization that by looking a second or third time at the same part of a lesson and by changing words with positive connotations into words with negative connotations and vice versa, you can alter the facts themselves as well as your interpretation. And perhaps you will become more conscious of the way in which your beliefs cause you to be selective in your retrieval of facts both during and after observations.

In my experience, it is impossible not to reflect personal beliefs at some level either in the recollections from a lesson, the notes taken during a lesson, or transcriptions or narrations from recordings. Nor can a person's values fail to show up in the use of these recollections, notes, transcriptions, and narrations. If the goal was to involve the class, an observer will more likely notice communications that he or she thinks show involvement rather than estrangement. If you know that the objective was to teach how to balance chemical formulas, as you listen to a recording of the lesson, your concentration on comments about chemical formulas may prevent you from hearing comments to the class to be quiet, descriptive information about elements, words of astonishment, excitement, or bewilderment.

Bateson makes the point this way: "But what gets to consciousness is selected; it is a systematic (not random) sampling of the rest. . . . I, the conscious I, see an unconsciously edited version of a small percentage of what affects my retina. I am guided in my perception by *purposes*." (Bateson, 1972, p. 434)

This is not to say we should not try to relate what we see to our purposes or our beliefs. But by engaging in conversations such as those stimulated by the activity sections, we are likely to see how our goals and beliefs are both congruous, or matching, and incongruous with our practices and behaviors. We will be arguing about such congruence rather than how successful or unsuccessful we were.

We will be arguing about grouping what we have observed, how to select different facts to refute the judgments and interpretations we make, ways to make our negative interpretations positive, and different types of transcription and narrations, rather than about the greater validity of our interpretations and judgments over those of others. The process of matching words, meanings, and interpretations defuses the temptation to engage in power play. The matching can enable us to play with the communications the way we played with the stamps when we grouped them in a range of ways.

Activity 14

Before turning to the specific classroom situations we will talk about in Part Two, take this opportunity to record a lesson in a manner other than your usual one. If you have not habitually taken notes during observation, write notes during a short segment of your observation and tape-record the lesson as well. After the observation, transcribe some of the exchanges from the tape, exactly as the words were said. After you have done that, listen again, and in brackets add other features to the words. Compare your notes and both types of transcriptions. Group some communications in a range of ways, related to goals, or to your beliefs.

If you are used to writing copious notes, go into a class without anything to write with or on. Just sit and observe. After the class write some notes about the lesson.

In either case, with a partner characterize the data you have and group the data in a range of ways. Ask which items are facts, which judgments, which explanations, or other types of words you use to characterize what you see. See how facts are selected to support interpretations, judgments, or the intentions set out for the lesson. See how close you come to feeling the way a police lieutenant did, in *Who Killed Palomino Molero?* by the Peruvian novelist Mario Vargas Llosa, as he was asked by one of his police officers if he knew everything about a murder they were both investigating: "Nothing's easy, Lituma," he answered. "The truths that seem most truthful, if you look at them from all sides, if you look at them close up, turn out either to be half truths or lies." (Vargas Llosa, 1986, p. 86)

CONVERSATIONS ABOUT TEACHING: A REVIEW

CONVERSATIONS ARE NOT BLACK AND WHITE

In my experience, the contrasting conversations that the activities in this book are supposed to lead to, do not suddenly begin. When I have analyzed my own conversations and those of others, I have seen examples of the usual conversations as well as examples of contrasting conversations.

Activity 15

In the scene that follows, there are some comments that exemplify the usual conversations and some that exemplify the contrasting conversations I am inviting you to try in this book. Please write *c c* next to those lines that you think exemplify contrasting conversations. Write *u c* next to those you think exemplify the usual conversations after observing a lesson. Write a question mark if you think the comments have features of both types of conversations, or if you cannot fit the comments neatly into either the usual or the contrasting conversations.

Given that one feature of contrasting conversations is that they require multiple interpretations, you may decide to put question marks next to each line in the conversation rather than use *u c* or *c c* to make any black-and-white grouping. The meaning of the words of course can be interpreted in many ways, especially since the conversation is taken out of context and consists of separate comments made at different times but consolidated below. Additionally, we each may see the lines in relationship to recent experiences similar to the ones discussed.

But when I invite you to write *u c* or *c c*, I am asking you to indicate the tendency, the direction that the line seems to be taking rather than in terms of absolutes. Consider *u c* and *c c* at opposite ends of a continuum and then decide whether you would put the line closer to either end of the continuum. The question mark can be used for those items that seem to be in the middle. Thus, as always, there is not a right answer for any of the items. Selecting one answer rather than another does, however, provide a means to make some of the features of the usual conversations and the contrasting conversations more explicit.

The speaker who observed the lesson is indicated by "v t," for visiting teacher. The speaker who taught the lesson is indicated by "t t," which stands for teaching teacher.

---

1. v t: What are you going to do about their mistakes?
   t t: Good question. 1. ____

---

42 ■ Learning to Look

2. v t: I notice that you're making me do all the thinking today.
   t t: (smiles and laughs)   2. ___

3. v t: I didn't like your first activity.   3. ___

4. t t: Do you think I should be more enthusiastic?   4. ___

5. t t: When I raise my voice, they always stop talking.   5. ___

6. t t: Today, I wrote clearly and neatly and in large letters. Tomorrow, I plan to write with very small letters. And I will write all over so that the board looks messy.   6. ___

7. v t: Though the change you tried was to say no after each student made an error, I noticed that you also shook your head sideways as you said it. And you moved closer to the students as well. Sometimes you smiled as you said no.   7a. ___
   t t: I noticed that when I said no, the students rewrote the sentence that I had dictated and showed it to me. In fact, the more I said no to each student, the more each student seemed to try again and again to get the sentence right!   7b. ___

8. v t: Tomorrow, when you are on hall duty and you see a student wearing a cap, instead of saying "Please take off your hat," say "Hide your hat or you'll lose it!"   8. ___

9. v t: Why did you spend so much time asking the students questions like this: "What is velocity?" "Define gravity." "Who knows the speed of light?"   9. ___

10. v t: What are some other ways to get them involved?   10. ___

Thinking about the Alternatives

Compare your labeling of the lines with your partner's. If you have the time, give your reasons for your choices even in instances where you agree. By comparing reasons, perhaps you will see other features of the lines that you did not notice when you first labeled them. In fact, there can be many reasons for writing u c, c c, or a question mark next to the lines.

The labels several other teachers and I used and some of the reasons for them are printed below, in case you would like to compare your answers or your partner's with those of others, or if you were not able to find

Conversations about Teaching: A Review ■ 43

a partner for this activity. The labels below are not the "right" labels but simply ones that I and others have attached to the lines. The reasons given are not to prove that the labels we used are correct but rather to show the direction of our of thinking, to show how we arrived at them. They represent explanations, not justifications.

1. When the teaching teacher says "good question" to refer to the visiting teacher's question in item 1, a u c is appropriate if you consider the words "good question" a judgment. If you consider the words simply a way to keep the conversation going—"I heard you, let's continue"—then a c c is appropriate.

2. If the teaching teacher is in fact trying to get the visiting teacher to "do all the thinking," then a u c is necessary since one goal of contrasting conversations is to jointly share feelings and interpretations. A c c fits if the teaching teacher is saying the words ironically and reminding both participants that the idea is for each to share, with no person in charge.

3. It is hard to see how "I didn't like your first activity" can be interpreted as anything but a judgment being made by the visiting teacher, so a u c is required. If you can see a way that the words "I didn't like your first activity" can be used to explore alternatives, then of course a c c can be written.

4. A c c fits if the teaching teacher is asking whether more enthusiasm should be tried to contrast more enthusiasm with less enthusiasm, and both the teaching teacher and the visiting teacher are exploring the various meanings of enthusiasm as well as the disadvantages and advantages observed of various amounts of teacher enthusiasm. The question can be seen as on the c c end of the continuum. But if the teaching teacher is thinking in terms of simple causation (changing A will alter or directly improve B), then we are moving in the direction of the u c end of the continuum.

5. "When I raise my voice they always stop talking" refers to one dimension of a communication. In addition, the comment suggests that one action directly causes another action. The use of "always" suggests a level of knowledge about complex human interaction that is hard to accept. "Most of the time" or even "almost always" would suggest a general tendency, without claiming a result that is very difficult to support.

Though many activities in this book require that communications be divided into two groups, suggesting a world in which everything can be neatly divided into watertight compartments or that all communications are either black or white, you are in fact asked to recategorize after each categorization. The point of the regrouping is to show that in fact any groupings we make are not watertight. The regroupings are meant to show that shades of grays more accurately represent reality than do black and white. Because of the apparent belief implied in this comment that one cause produces one result and that we can predict outcomes with absolute assurance—always—I would label the line u c. Or, to remind us all of the limitation of absolute groupings, we could say that the word "always" makes the comment fit toward the u c end of a continuum. At the same time, the words "raise my voice" and "stop talking" can be seen as attempts to be specific and therefore move the comment towards the c c end of the continuum.

6. The prescription by the teaching teacher to him- or herself in line 6 merits a c c if the prescription is given as a means to compare two practices. If, after the teaching teacher writes in a messy way, he or she concludes that neat writing is always superior, the teaching teacher would be moving towards the u c end of the continuum. "Always superior" is saying that one practice is in all cases better than another. Such a conclusion ignores the possibility that as we engage in an activity over and over, the power of the activity might decrease. Finally, the comment seems to be one-dimensional and does not in any way suggest playing with alternative interpretations of what we see. If intended in this way, it belongs at the u c end of the continuum.

7a. The visiting teacher uses words that suggest that he or she believes each communication is part of a network. The word *no* is discussed in relationship to gestures—shaking the head sideways and smiling—and movement—getting closer to the students. Consequently, my partner and I put a c c for 7a.

7b. The teaching teacher precedes his or her claim about students trying harder with the word "seemed," showing a tentativeness characteristic of contrasting conversations. But the teaching teacher limits the discussion of the use of *no* to one result—trying harder to get it right. Consequently, my partner and I both wrote a u c for the teaching teacher's comments.

A c c could be used for the teaching teacher's comments if the teaching teacher would have mentioned other results, such as these likely ones: "Some of the students seemed to act the same way today that they always do. When I looked at the tape the second time, I noticed that Catherine put her hands to her eyes after I said no to her—she seemed quite hurt." But suggesting that the use of *no* has only one set of consequences for all students is a bit of a generalization, even when tempered with "seemed" and thus shows at the minimum a movement towards the u c end of the continuum.

8. The visiting teacher's advice about hall duty could hardly be more prescriptive. In isolation, it sounds just like "I'll show you how to teach!" and thus needs to be labeled u c. If, on the other hand, the prescription is being given in order to compare two practices, to explore the results of two different ways of

dealing with school rules, then the prescription can be labeled c c. So, outside of the context of this book, in isolation, the command is an example of the usual conversation. In the context of this book, it could be an example of a contrasting conversation.

9. When I ask questions to interrogate, to force a person to justify a practice, to give reasons for having done something, I am acting as if I am in charge. When I ask questions out of curiosity, because an explanation would help me understand, I am acting either as an equal or a person in a learner's position. If the visiting teacher is asking the teaching teacher a question as a peer, then a c c seems reasonable. If the visiting teacher is asking the teaching teacher as a person in charge, a u c seems reasonable. Given the lack of context for the questions in 9, a question mark seems reasonable.

On the other hand, even without more context, a tendency towards the u c end of the continuum could be argued because whether I ask for justification or an explanation, I assume that teachers can explain what they do. One of the assumptions underlying contrasting conversations is that we are *not* always conscious of everything we do. As a result, asking for explanations contradicts one of the ideas behind contrasting conversations. Explanations can of course reveal values that are held. If the visiting teacher is asking the teaching teacher for reasons so both can see the values held by the teaching teacher, it could be argued that there is movement toward the c c end of the continuum. But the lines in 9 give no evidence of this aim, and so again a question mark is probably most reasonable.

10. A central feature of contrasting conversations is specificity. Using this criterion, the visiting teacher's question in 10 has to be labeled u c. Another reason for labeling it u c concerns the issue of building alternatives on observed practices and comparing subsequent alternatives with the previously observed practices. There is no way to compare alternatives with the observed practices if a visiting teacher is simply asking a teaching teacher who has been visited to think of alternatives, without reference to some excerpts from the observed lesson.

Optional Activity: Images of Conversations

If you would like to illustrate features of both the usual and the contrasting conversations by drawing images, turn to Activity 15A in the appendix.

LOOKING AT OUR OWN CONVERSATIONS

Contrasting conversations don't just suddenly start. Most conversations contain various proportions of statements and questions we would call usual and contrasting. Just as we cannot understand our own teaching without some analysis of excerpts from our lessons, so we cannot know the extent to which we are changing the ways we talk about teaching without looking.

In some of the activities in Part Two of this book, you will often be engaged in contrasting conversations because the activities are designed to produce them. In order to see the extent to which your conversations that are unrelated to specific activities contain elements associated with contrasting conversations, I have developed Activity 16. It can be used as both a review of Part One and a monitor of the dialogs you have about beliefs and teaching practices separate from the activities in this book.

Activity 16

Below I have listed a number of features of the usual conversations and contrasting conversations, as I describe them. Record one or two discussions that you and a colleague have about classes you have observed. Select a minute or two of the tape. Select some of the pairs of features below. Then replay the section you are analyzing and write down lines from the conversations that match the headings in the series of pairs you have selected. As you see, there are blank lines in the last two pairs for you and your partner to generate your own features.

general	specific

intuitive with analysis	intuitive without analysis

drastic changes suggested	small changes suggested

judgmental to evaluate	judgmental to explore

single causation	multiple causation

cliches used	new terms used

comments made about short excerpts	comments made about entire lesson

evaluative comments	descriptive comments

Thinking about the Alternatives

A low number of comments in any column is no cause for alarm nor jubilation. The amount will simply show what you are doing. If you find only "specific comments," then you are incorporating one feature of contrasting conversations in your conversations. If you find only "general comments," you are not. By changing some of your general comments to specific comments perhaps you will be able to generate some specific comments for your next conversation.

The number of features of the usual or contrasting conversations is only one index of what you are doing as you are discussing lessons you observe. Remember, having contrasting conversations is not an end in itself, but a means to another end. In the following dialog between Gregory Bateson and his daughter, this end of contrasting conversations is described:

> DAUGHTER: But Daddy, you said all conversation is only telling other people that you are not angry with them....
>
> FATHER: Did I? No—not all conversation, but much of it. Sometimes, if people are willing to listen carefully, it is possible to do more than exchange greetings and good wishes. Even to do more than exchange information. *The two people may even find out something which neither of them knew before.*
>
> (Bateson, 1972, p. 12, italics added)

The "much of it" in the father's first line reminds us of the continuum. The "sometimes" and "possible" bring to mind the tentative, exploratory nature of contrasting conversations. The "all" in the daughter's first line reminds both Bateson and us of the danger of absolutes. The last line states the potential of the conversations you can have, not only as you engage in the activities in Part Two, but also—and more importantly—in your own conversations when you are not doing the activities in this book.

*I*MPLICATIONS OF CONTRASTING CONVERSATIONS

As people read books, they often highlight sentences with a felt-tip pen. To conclude our review, I've listed some excerpts from the Introduction and Part One that various readers have highlighted. When I highlight items, I think of implications the words have. Thus I have written one of many possible implications after each excerpt.

> "In the ... conversations that will emerge from the activities in this book, some evaluations will be replaced by descriptions and analyses ... cut-and-dried advice to solve a perceived problem will be replaced by *multiple interpretations* of what is observed" (p. 1).
>
> *Implication:* We don't know what good teaching is. As soon as we think we have found it, we will realize that we and those we teach have changed, and consequently we need to engage in different practices.
>
> "And the exploration of relationships between what is observed,

what is said and done, and what had been intended will be carried out" (p. 1).

Implication: Because we are often unaware of our beliefs and unconscious of many of our teaching practices, there is sometimes a mismatch between them.

"With nothing to 'prove,' both participants can move freely, as in struggle. Neither one is engaging in a power struggle where one gives advice to the other or evaluates and judges the other" (pp. 1–2).

Implication: We can generate alternative practices with our peers without worrying about failing, putting on a poor show, or having to assert our ideas.

"Conclusions . . . from their explorations up to this point include: . . . Multiple analyses of small amounts of data can reveal a great deal; even data that we think have only two or three features often have many, many more" (p. 26).

Implication: Teaching practices are patterned in systematic ways, just as is discourse in other settings. We follow sociolinguistic rules in classrooms just as we follow such rules in all settings. No one trains either teachers or emcees on television game shows to signal transitions to new topics or activities by saying, "O.K., now . . ." just as no one trains us to slow down our speaking rate when talking to babies. (The usual conversations of course provide another illustration of discourse patterned in systematic ways.)

"The activities of this book are expressly designed to free us in our observing, our thinking, and our teaching practices."

Implication: The delight, joy, and freedom that result from invention and improvisation in music, art, writing, and scientific experiment and speculation is available to us as teachers.

"Dialogs in which we describe and analyze are important, but without action they are insufficient. As you see different characteristics of teaching practices in classes and discuss them, I will invite, request, or prescribe a change in some practice in a subsequent class" (p. 7).

Implication: Exploration of our beliefs and teaching practices requires more than conversations; alternative teaching practices must be tried.

"The dialogs you will have with your partner, and with yourself, and the various alternatives you will use in your teaching are not the ends, but the means to understanding your teaching and to discovering new ideas. By constantly considering practices and results you consider negative in a positive way, and vice versa, your beliefs about the values of different practices and results will change. You will learn how to compare options in new ways" (p. 7).

Implication: Accepting our day-to-day explanations for our own successes and failures and for our own diagnoses of their causes is based on the unproven assumption that relationships among communications are clear-cut and what appears to us is the only reality. Since our treatments for failures often develop from our own diagnoses, misdiagnoses can lead only to mistreatment.

"The grouping activities illustrated the fact that the theories of the world that allow us to cope with reality also trap us——Looking at the postage rate is important for getting the mail through, but while focusing on the rate we fail to see the figure or the caption or the design or the date" (p. 27).

Implication: It is obvious that comments we make about what we see reveal our beliefs—our perceptions of reality—as much as what is being observed. But seeing what is obvious, much less acting on or noticing what we take for granted, is difficult and probably infrequent.

"We will be arguing about grouping what we have observed, how to select different facts to refute the judgments and interpretations we make, ways to make our negative interpretations positive, and different types of transcription and narrations, rather than about the greater validity of our interpretations and judgments over those of others. The process of matching words, meanings, and interpretations defuses the temptation to engage in power play. The matching can enable us to play with the communications the way we played with the stamps when we grouped them in a range of ways" (pp. 40–41).

Implication: We are capable of much more than we often believe we are.

"a small change in the way we greet students might affect how we deal with comprehension in a profound way. It is in the classroom as it is in the ecology of the world outside: Diverse forms of life and activity are interrelated and interdependent. For example, a slight increase in the number of cattle that graze in a dry area can increase the rate of erosion in geometric proportions" (p. 6).

Implication: To explore our beliefs and teaching practices, there is no need to make drastic or large changes; all that is needed are small changes: giving students 3 seconds to respond rather than 1; asking a question with genuine interest rather than with a neutral tone of voice.

Other implications for each excerpt are, of course, possible. Perhaps one of the most crucial is the fact that each person will write personal implications which are likely to differ in many ways from each other person's list. Yet, at the same time, within each ramification from each person, there will be much overlap and many similarities.

Optional Activity: Additional Implications

In the appendix appears Activity 16A to provide you with another way to explore what we have learned.

PART TWO Applications of Observing

CHOICES IN EXPLORATIONS

As you will recall from the Introduction to this book, the topics in Part Two are arranged in alphabetical order. This approach has been chosen to remind you that throughout the workshop which this book presents the goal is to engage in a process, not to complete a lockstep series of sequential exercises to master information per se. Consequently, you are free to select the sequence you wish to follow in Part Two. There is no need to start with a particular topic because the topics are not the ends. They are the means to the end of illustrating ways of exploring your beliefs and teaching practices. Whether you start with "Feedback" or "Starting Class," the activities will help you engage in contrasting conversations.

Another reason for encouraging choice is that this book is predicated on the belief that what we all do and think is related. As the Russian psychologist Vygotsky claimed, "Every thought tends to connect with something else, to establish a relationship between things. Every thought moves, grows, and develops." (Vygotsky, 1962, p. 125)

While you will be able to find some topics that treat matters with which you are concerned, it was not intended to imply that the topics treated are of central concern to all teachers. Indeed, one premise of this book is that teachers will collaborate in the selection of both the topics to explore and the classes to describe and analyze. What you have in your hands is not a package of information but a workshop with a variety of activities to choose from.

COMMUNICATIONS WITHOUT LANGUAGE

Recently, I was called for jury duty. During the jury selection process on a case that was going to involve child witnesses, the prosecuting attorney asked potential jurors how they determined whether a child was lying or telling the truth. The first few people who were asked all said something like "By the way they look and act." They all said that to determine whether a person was truthful or not, whether adult or child, they observed the individual's body language.

Whether the "body language test" is accurate or not, I cannot say. The lawyers both for the prosecution and the defense did not invite those who said they could determine truth by noting how a person looked to serve on the jury. But there is no doubt that how we move and look does affect others.

UNCONSCIOUS AND CONSCIOUS COMMUNICATIONS

The descriptions under "Body Language as Detail," taken from *Maigret and the Millionaires*, one of George Simenon's detective stories involving Inspector Maigret, contain some examples of body language.

Body Language as Detail

1 Automatically, out of sheer curiosity, the superintendent reached out to touch the
2 chain, and just as he did so, the man Arnold turned toward him with a severe
3 look, as though to accuse him of unseemly or indelicate behavior.

4 It was all done much more subtly than by words, with just a glance, barely
5 insistent, and a scarcely perceptible change of expression.
6 Then Maigret dropped the chain and assumed an attitude of which he promptly
7 felt ashamed, since it was that of a guilty man.

8 Had Lapointe really noticed this, and averted his eyes on purpose?

9 Her hands, which looked older than her face, were twitching nervously, and she
10 was wringing her fingers, leaving white marks over the knuckles.

11 It was Lapointe who noticed that the superintendent, as he went by, laid his
12 hand for an instant, as though absent-mindedly, on John Arnold's shoulder; and
13 the young policeman's eyes took on a troubled look as they followed his chief to
14 the door.

(Simenon, 1974, pp. 27, 169)

In some mystery stories, the body language is noted to present clues to help solve a mystery rather than to provide details. You can see some clues in the descriptions in the following excerpt.

Body Language as a Clue

1 They said when they found the seaman, he was huddled in the embryo position,
2 his hands clasped round the gunny sack, which was pressed into his belly. The
3 phrase Craig used was that he seemed to be "protecting it like a baby."

4 Preston could see the oddity. If a man is being kicked half to death, the instinct
5 is to roll into a ball, like Semyonov [had done and] . . . to use the hands to protect
6 the head. Why would a man take the force of the kicks on an unprotected head
7 in order to guard a worthless canvas bag [held with his hands over his
8 stomach]?

(Forsyth, 1984, p. 319)

We can apply what we learned about the grouping process to study these descriptions. You may want to reread the two selections before starting Activity 1.

Applications of Observing

| Activity 1 | Copy in the left-hand column those words or phrases from the excerpt that suggest that the body language used (either to add detail or provide clues) seems unconscious or automatic. In the right-hand column, write the words that you think suggest that the body language is deliberate and conscious. |

unconscious	conscious
turned toward	*reached out to touch*
twitch	*severe look*
	dropped... assumed
	averted
	wringing
	loud hand

Thinking about the Alternatives

Here are words that others wrote in the left-hand column because they imply or explicitly indicate unconscious behavior.

From the first excerpt:

automatically (1)
felt ashamed (7)
twitching nervously (9)
as though absent-mindedly (12)
troubled look (13)

From the second excerpt:

instinct (4)

Some people listed the following words in the right-hand column because they thought that they might signal conscious body language.

From the first excerpt:

turned toward him with a severe look ... to accuse him (2 and 3)
It was all done (4)
dropped the chain (6)
assumed an attitude (6)
averted his eyes on purpose (8)
who noticed (11)

From the second excerpt:

found the seaman (1)
take the force of the kicks (6)

| Activity 2 | Observe a person you are working with, either live or a video recording, during a lesson. You may want to observe yourself teaching on a videotape. Having some pictures taken during a class is another way to collect samples of gestures you or a person you are working with use. From the live observations, videotape, or photographs, write down descriptions of some behaviors you note, or draw sketches of them. Then, copy a few of them in one of the columns in Activity 1, above. |

Communications without Language ■ 55

Thinking about the Alternatives

When some people try to place sketches or descriptions of their own behavior under the unconscious/conscious columns, they begin to think that the dichotomy is not as clear as they initially thought. Some of them begin to wonder not only about their own actions but those of others as well. Rereading the excerpts from Simenon's mystery, some people ask whether it was possible that the woman whose hands were "twitching nervously" was in fact deliberately manipulating her hands because she wanted those observing her to think that she was nervous.

In fact, removing the prefix un- from the left column heading and placing it in the right column heading would enable us to realize that it is possible to argue that each of the behaviors we considered unconscious could have been deliberate. When two people walking down the street move their legs in unison, they might not think about their synchronization but, if asked, might be very aware of it. When we see a student jiggling keys, we might think the student is deliberately trying to annoy us or the class. Yet there is the possibility that the student is unaware that he or she is holding the keys, let alone jiggling them to produce noise.

As we observe gestures we consider unconscious, trying to generate reasons to support the removal of the prefix un- from our labeling of the gestures may lead to a new understanding of ways we all communicate with our bodies.

ANALYZING COMMUNICATIONS WITHOUT LANGUAGE

Because of the central importance of communications without language—of movements, gestures, and looks we give others—the remaining activities in this section are devoted to the observation and analysis of these nonverbal communications. Elsewhere in this book we have been considering and "playing" with words people say as represented in transcriptions. Now you will be able to play with body language as represented in photographs. While photos make this static and thus different from body language seen live or on videotapes shown with the sound off, the processes we use to analyze the communications are similar.

Activity 3

On the blank line underneath the photograph, write a title for the picture. It's worth repeating here that there are no wrong answers for the activities in this book.

Title: _An Interview_

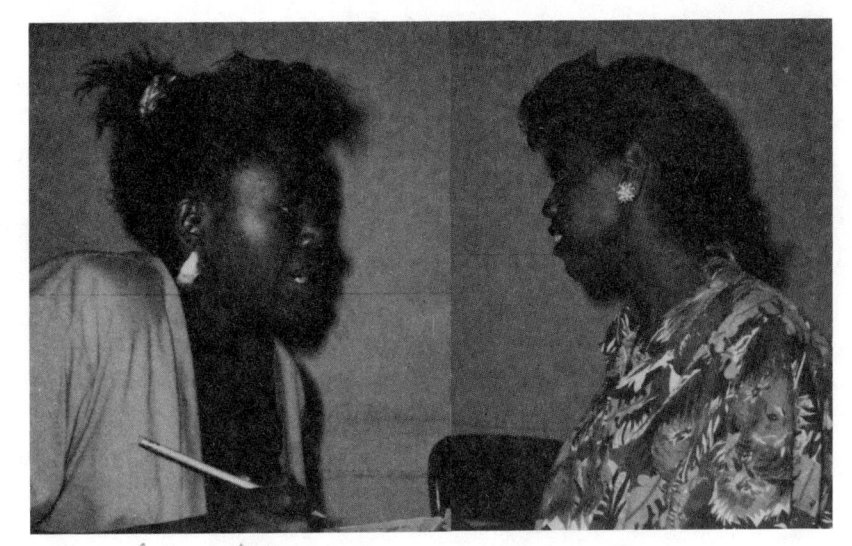

Compare your title with your partner's, or with these that others gave, below:

- Striking earrings
- Intimate conversation
- Friends
- Shadows
- Out of sync

> Now list some items in the photo that you believe led you to come up with your title. Feel free to add items that you did not originally notice but that you now see as more evidence for your original title.
>
> _two people looking at each other_
> _pen & paper_
> _sitting down_
> _poised to write_
>
> Also look for evidence that your original title might not, upon re-examination, reflect the picture as accurately as you first thought.
>
> _type of room -- classroom_
> _clothing_
> _earrings, hair scrunchi_
> _shadows_

Communications without Language ■ 57

Thinking about the Alternatives

Below is a list of what others have said led to the titles they selected, or that on a second, third, or fourth look seemed to suggest a title different from the first one they had suggested.

> Striking earrings: The earrings just stood out-they seemed so bright, especially against the black skins. I see shadows now and the hair tie on the person on the left; I missed these on the first look.
>
> Intimate conversation: The eyes of each person seem to be staring very intently at the other person. The two people are close to each other, though neither actually seems to be talking as I look again.
>
> Friends: The mouth positions seem to be almost mirrors of each other, they seem to be looking at each other without embarrassment so they must know each other.
>
> Shadows: I noticed the chin on the person on the right, but it was too big in relationship to the face, so I then realized it must be a shadow. Then, I looked at the person on the left and saw the profile of the face-just like a silhouette-on the wall. The hair on the person on the right seems to be a shadow, but it might be the hair is slightly out of focus-but the size of the chin is what got me thinking shadows from the beginning.
>
> Out of sync: The eyes don't really connect. Each seems to be in a different place.

ADJUSTING OUR PERCEPTIONS

The words Simenon and Forsyth use in the excerpts in Activity 1 describe the body language they want to portray, the words used to give titles to the photograph, and the words used to note the items that you noticed in the photograph all have something in common. The words both authors used, like the words we use, are based on our perceptions of the meanings of the body language we see. Once we start stating what we perceive, we seem quite capable of finding evidence to support our initial perception.

Cervantes illustrates ways our perceptions filter reality over and over in *Don Quixote*. One classic example occurs when Don Quixote visits an inn, early in his travels. Given Don Quixote's preconceived notions, based on his readings, that the world operates following the rules of chivalry and that he is a knight errant, the sequence below is not strange. Rather, it describes how we all behave when we observe what others are doing.

Don Quixote's Glasses

As everything that our adventurer thought, saw, or imagined seemed to follow the fashion of his reading [about knighthood], as soon as he saw the inn he convinced himself that it was a fortress with its four towers and pinnacles of shining silver, complete with a draw-bridge, a deep moat and all those appurtenances with which such castles are painted. So he approached the inn, which to his mind was a castle, and when still a short distance away reined Rocinante in, expected some dwarf to mount the battlements and sound a trumpet to announce that a knight was approaching the fortress. But when he saw that there was some delay, and that Rocinante was in a hurry to get to the stable, he went up to the inn door and, seeing the two young women standing there, took them for two beauteous maidens or graceful ladies taking the air at the castle gate. Now at that very moment, as chance would have it, a swineherd was collecting from the stubble a drove of hogs—pardon me for naming them—and blew his horn to call them together. But Don Quixote immediately interpreted this in his own way, as some dwarf giving notice of his approach....

While they were thus occupied there happened to come to the inn a hog-gelder, and as he arrived he blew his reed whistle four or five times; which finally convinced Don Quixote that he was at some famous castle, that they were entertaining him with music, that the pollack was trout, the black bread of the whitest flour, the whores ladies and the innkeeper warden of the castle.

(pt. 1, chap. 2)

The potential jurors who thought that children who did not look at them when they spoke were telling lies were no different from Don Quixote. The jurors, Don Quixote, and the rest of us all have an idea of what goes on in the world according to our perceptions. Then we see evidence that *fits in* with our perception, partly because the "glasses" we wear filter reality. Just as some of the gestures we make are not conscious ones, so the process of selecting bits of reality to fit our perceptions is probably unconscious.

To illustrate how our "glasses" filter reality from time to time, I will narrate the way I collected body language during oral reading lessons for many years.

I instructed video technicians to zero in on the heads of students as they read orally. In particular, I was looking to see whether a reader looked down at the material being read to read it silently and then looked up to say orally what had just been read silently. I was interested in eye contact between the reader and the person the reader was saying the lines to. I was also interested in seeing whether the eyes of the reader rolled upwards as the reader said the words aloud. As some potential jurors think that lack of eye contact suggests dishonesty, I believed that rolling eyes upwards as a person says something that has just been read silently is a signal of an attempt to recall words rather than an attempt to convey meaning. Rolling eyes suggested to me memorization and word-calling rather than expression of meaning.

Well, it turns out that one day, the threaded device that held the video camera in position—so that heads could be captured—was not tightened. So during the entire videotaping not one head was collected! No eye contact, no rolling eyes! The video camera had slipped down and was consequently pointed at an angle that revealed only arms, hands, and feet, no heads and no eyes. I started to look at the tape anyway. And as I and others looked and listened, we began to notice that as a person was reading orally, or saying the words orally that had been just read silently, the person would often punctuate the air with an arm or leg at the exact moment when he or she paused at the end of a group of words that constituted a breath or a sense group.

My usual method of collecting body language—aiming only at

heads—had obscured data that revealed the same phenomenon. We saw that in many instances word-calling was distinguished from saying word groups or sense groups with expression by the movement of the readers' hands, arms, or feet, not just the readers' eyes.

As we looked at arms and hands rather than heads, we also grouped the communications we saw in a range of ways. We wrote examples of what we saw under these pairs: *words alone/words with movement; attention to the form of the words/attention to the meaning of the words*. We noted that when the person who asked the readers to read corrected pronunciation, there was hardly any movement on the part of the readers, no body language. Readers held the book with both hands or held the book with one hand and pointed to the words with the other. When readers' pronunciation was not corrected but comments about the meaning of the lines were made, a reader held the book with one hand and moved the other hand in a variety of ways. Some readers cut the air gently at the end of each breath or sense group. Others paused after a word, reread words before the pause, and as they reread moved their hands as if they were keeping time to some unheard music.

I now look at heads *and* arms *and* feet to see the extent to which a person seems to be reading to express meaning rather than to pronounce the words correctly, with or without understanding. Looking at more than the eyes and head has revealed something I had not seen before. Looking with a different pair of glasses enabled/freed/forced me to see something I had not seen before.

Another instance of changing glasses came about when I was looking at a television program called "The Honeymooners," starring Jackie Gleason. I was able to see a different vision of reality this time not as a result of a broken video camera but because of the use of two pairs of columns, two T's, to represent two pairs of contrasting features of the body language I saw. The first pair of features I used was *silence/talking*. I saw silences that I had seen many times before, but the silences revealed nothing new. Then, someone set up a pair of columns entitled *opening of a new scene/after opening of a new scene*. The body language we noted under *opening of a new scene* was never accompanied by any words. The communications we noted under *opening of a new scene* were the same ones that we had listed under *silence*. The body language we noted under *after opening of a new scene* was usually the same body language we noted in the column under the heading *talking*.

During the opening silence, a single character usually appeared and spent some seconds in the scene, which was usually the kitchen of an apartment, walking around, arranging the tablecloth on the kitchen table, unpacking a bag of groceries, checking a pan on the stove, turning the water faucet to be sure it was off, checking to be sure the gas was off, or some similar activity. It seemed that each character spent some time using body language without speaking at the beginning of each scene.

Why the characters acted as they did we cannot be sure. How conscious they were of their silent actions we cannot know for certain. Perhaps they were getting ready to say the lines by rehearsing them in their minds, or perhaps they were allowing both the studio audience and the television audience to settle down so that the first lines could be heard. Or perhaps they needed time to create the mood they desired. Or perhaps

Applications of Observing

they were simply following unconscious patterns.

But whatever the reasons, the silence we noticed in a television drama I have never observed during the presentation of dialogs in classrooms. As soon as students are told to start a dialog, they do. They do not pause before speaking. Collecting different data using a different lens, filter, or frame showed some data that we had not seen through scores of previous viewings and generated an alternative that can be tried when doing dialogs in a class.

Activity 4

On the lines below, describe how your preconceived notion of the meaning of some body language was once changed as a result of some experience or some grouping exercise, so that you can share with another how you were able to move from seeing through one pair of glasses to seeing through another pair.

An example written by another person is presented below the blank lines so that you and your partner can compare your thoughts with those of a third person.

> **A Time When I Changed "Glasses"**
>
> ? One day when I was riding a subway train, a man came into the car asking for money. He had a full length cast on his leg, which made feel sympathy for him. Then I noticed that the cast was on over his clothes. Undoubtedly, this forced me to question whether he was indeed homeless and hungry or wanting money for other reasons. It also made me wonder if he put the cast on himself (and if others noticed the discrepancy) and whether he was really injured.

An interesting ex. (We sure get to do a lot of hypothesizing in N.Y.C. Don't we?)

One day, when I stopped my car at a traffic light, I noticed a creature with beautiful blond hair sitting on the passenger side of the car in front of me. I wanted to see if the face matched the beautiful hair. After the traffic light changed to green, I maneuvered my car through traffic to get alongside the car with the creature with the beautiful blond hair. As I turned my head to the left to look at the passenger, I was surprised to see a panting Afghan dog!

HOW WE EDIT OUR OBSERVATIONS

The pictures of the two people shown in Activity 3 were in fact cut from two separate pictures, which are shown below. Cropping, or editing, of pictures is common in moviemaking, television program development, yearbook production, and other endeavors that require body language to be rearranged to illustrate a message we want to communicate.

Similarly, we rearrange language when we edit and rewrite words. Not

Picture 1

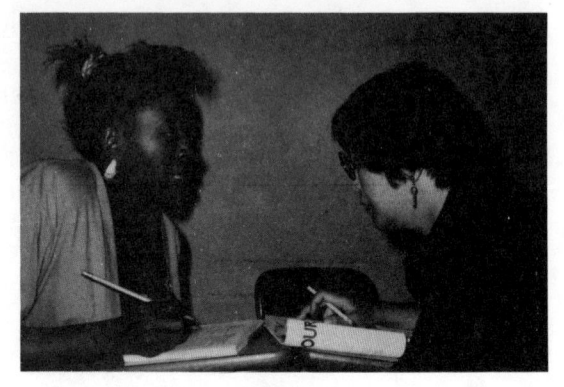

Picture 2

only do we each seem to wear glasses to filter reality to match our notions in whatever medium we happen to be using during editing, but it can be argued that when we look at two people interacting, we are cropping and editing their body language live!

The combining of pictures that I accomplished with scissors and glue to produce the photograph in Activity 3 is a conscious act similar to the unconscious acts we each perform when we look at what is before us.

Activity 5

Below, write in the left-hand column reasons the two people in each photograph shown here are connecting with their body language. In the right-hand column, write down what shows that the two people in each picture are not connecting with their body language.

Picture 1	connecting	not connecting
	eye contact	distance
	smile	

Picture 2	connecting	not connecting
	leaning forward	(R) pt. to something on paper
		eye contact?

62 ■ Applications of Observing

Thinking about the Alternatives

By remembering the potential jurors who were so convinced they could determine whether a person was speaking the truth or not by a person's body language, you will be reminded of the fact that there are no right or wrong groupings. Rather, the groupings we each make simply reflect the perceptions we have and the glasses we are using. By comparing our groupings with those others have made, we can perhaps see possible connections and lack of connections that we had not previously seen because we'll be changing glasses.

The way I cut off the person on the left of Picture 1 and the right of Picture 2 and juxtaposed them to form the composite in Activity 3 reveals my preconceived notions of what connecting means. Eye contact is a criterion I use for determining being connected; whether eye contact actually signals being connected or not is a separate issue. So, using this criterion, the pair in Picture 1 seems to be connecting more than the pair in Picture 2. If we look at the position of the lips, the pair in Picture 1 both seem to be smiling. Only the person on the left in Picture 2 seems to be smiling. So on a second dimension, the pair in Picture 1 seem to be connecting more. On the other hand, the pencils in the hands of both readers in Picture 2 are almost at the same angle—an unconscious connection? And, if the person on the left of Picture 2 has just finished saying a line and the person on the right is restating the line while checking with the book, perhaps they have been intensely listening to each other.

The students in the pictures shown here had been instructed to read a passage in front of them silently and then look up and say the lines that they had just read to their partner. The goal was to say the lines while looking at another person rather than to say them while looking at the page of the material they were reading. This was a task few had ever done in their lives, so part of the "meaning" of their body language might be that each person was trying a type of reading not previously done.

The pair in Picture 2, who might seem to be connecting less than the pair in Picture 1, might be jointly learning and thus connecting in a way different from ways we might readily notice. By writing down reasons why those in the two pictures are connecting or not, you make conscious the criteria you use for determining how people connect.

The description of an incident between the police and a citizen in the story below reveals the danger of assuming that we can understand the meaning of body language based on our perceptions alone. The description also reveals one step we can take to decrease the danger.

Blind News

It seems that two police officers in Hayward, California, on May 16, 1989, beat a blind man with their batons after mistaking his collapsible cane for an illegal martial arts weapon. The blind man was waiting for a bus. The two police officers went up to him and said, "Please hand over the contents of your pockets."

The blind man did not see their uniforms since he was blind. The police officers did not know he was blind since he was looking right at them with his eyes open, and therefore did not identify themselves as police officers. The blind man thought that the two people who had demanded the contents of his pockets were thieves and therefore did not hand over the contents of his pockets.

The police officers hit the blind man on the legs and on the forearm in an attempt to "disarm" the blind man. The blind man thought he was being mugged, and the police officers thought the blind man was resisting arrest. At some point, an observer yelled, "He's blind!" The police officers regretted the incident.

Adapted from a news item

The three people directly involved in the incident and described in the previous news item each based their actions on an initial understanding, reading, or perception of the meaning of the body lanugage, or, in the case of the blind man, body language and spoken language of the others. In the end, the police were blind in their own way, for they did not see the same reality the blind man saw and felt he represented. Each party kept the same pair of glasses on until an outside observer with a different set of glasses shared his perception. The outsider's words, "He's blind!" enabled the police to change their lenses. Had another observer shouted, "They're police officers," the blind man would have had evidence that might have enabled him to change his.

Can you remember an incident where you acted like the police officers or the blind man?

Activity 6

As you can see in the six photographs reproduced here, these people appear to be engaged in what seem to be reading and writing activities. On your own, group the photos in at least four ways using the T's below. First, write the numbers of the pictures you think are in some way the same in the left column and those that are contrasting in the right column. Then, after you write titles for both the left and right columns of your first grouping, regroup the pictures on the basis of some other dimensions, or features, you notice in the photographs. For example, one dimension could be distance between eyes and reading material—close and far. After the pictures were grouped on this dimension, they could be regrouped on the basis of their position: standing while reading or writing versus sitting while reading and writing.

After you do your four groupings, compare them with those your partner has made. If you can, tape-record your discussion; there will be an opportunity to use this recording later in this section. If you cannot, try to note during this discussion the ways you each used similarities as well as differences in your groupings.

Picture 1

Picture 2

64 ■ Applications of Observing

Picture 3

Picture 4

Picture 5

Picture 6

| 1,4 alone | 2,5 together | 3 library | 1,2,4,5,6 classroom |

| 1,4,5,3 ♀>♂ | 2,6 ♂>♀ | 3,4,6 standing | 1,2,5 sitting |

Communications without Language ■ 65

Thinking about the Alternatives

Some titles generated by other people when sorting the photographs are listed below. Circle any of these titles that are the same as those you wrote. Do this in order to see the degree to which you noticed what others did. You will recall that when grouping stamps many people with diverse backgrounds generated some identical groupings. Many people categorized the stamps according to shape and postage rate, for example. Noticing when many people apply the same preconceived notions to the reality we observe can sometimes enable us to see our beliefs more clearly.

off task	on task		standing	sitting
silence	talking		classroom	non-classroom
necks straight	necks curved		taking in letters	producing letters
one person	more than one person		helping	not helping

In order to become more aware of the beliefs that enable us to determine by looking at others whether they are helping or not helping, on task or off task, connecting or not connecting, telling the truth or not telling the truth, switch columns with a partner. Try to see how what seem to be curved necks may in some way be straight. In pictures that show only one person try to see whether there is any evidence that suggests that the person who seems alone is in fact aware of others someplace around. Or, try to see how people sitting and standing, though having their legs in different positions, are similar in the way they are using other parts of their bodies. In short try to *reframe* each picture as Don Quixote reframed people and scenes he saw to fit his world of knights and chivalry.

On the blanks below, write down two pairs of titles you switched that revealed something you had not seen before. Select one pair of titles that require a bit of inference such as *off task/on task* and one that requires less inference such as *standing/sitting*. Write down some of the reasons you used to support your initial framings that after reconsideration turned out to provide support for opposite framings.

Applications of Observing

> *books and newspapers: in relation to classroom and non-classroom. I noticed the presence of different materials, i.e. prepared texts/books and 'italia'/newspapers*
>
> *off task and on task: in connection to the books and newspapers consideration needs to be given to whether these materials are being used by the students for leisure or classroom purposes.*

NOTING SIMILARITIES AND DIFFERENCES

We pause here to reflect on the thought processes that are used in grouping and on how these affect observations. When Vygotsky reflected on grouping activities, he had this to say about the process of sorting:

> Our own experimental studies suggest that the child becomes aware of differences earlier than of likenesses, not because differences lead to malfunctioning, but because awareness of similarity requires a more advanced structure of generalization and conceptualization than awareness of dissimilarity. In analyzing the development of concepts of difference and likeness, we found that consciousness of likeness presupposes the formation of a generalization, or of a concept, embracing the objects that are alike; consciousness of difference requires no such generalization—it may come about in other ways.
>
> (Vygotsky, 1962, pp. 88, 89)

During this workshop when you were asked to note similarities (such as circling titles of photographs you used that were the same as those that others used). The purpose was to remind you of the importance of seeing what various bits of data have in common. Otherwise, many of you may get the impression that grouping is designed only to highlight differences. But if we are to believe Vygotsky, seeing similarities—what Bronowski has called "hidden likenesses"—is equally important, and perhaps more difficult.

Activity 7

If you were able to tape-record your discussions of your grouping or regrouping of the photographs, listen to the recording. Note on the lines below the degree to which you, like Vygotsky, found it harder to note similarities than differences. If you were not able to tape-record, try to remember comments that you or the person you are working with made.

> **Similarities and differences**
>
> Based on our conversation, we felt that differences are more easily detected than similarities. Also, when looking for distinguishing characteristics there was the tendency to focus on one trait and its 'non'-trait. Why is that? Could it be a way of mental processing? A matter of socialization — that people tend to identify those which do not 'belong' to the group or share similar characteristics?

Some good Qs emerged from this

Another way to see the degree to which we notice similarities and differences is to note multiple features of the items we group. As you recall, we grouped stamps not only into the contrasting pairs of various postage rates but also on the basis of whether they fit pairs such as *air mail/non-air mail, with clouds/without clouds,* and so forth. As we continued to look, we realized that additional categories highlighted additional features of each stamp, features we initially did not see. Categories such as *patriotic symbols, water, flora,* and *sources of heat,* all enabled us to see even more features of each stamp.

So for example, if you grouped Pictures 1, 2, 3, and 5 under *necks curved* and also grouped them all under *on task,* you would see that one signal of being on task for you is posture. Seeing that 1 and 5 fit under *sitting* and 3 and 4 under *standing* might make you realize another facet of posture that previously you had not associated with being on task. If you placed all the pictures under *on task,* then you might have some features that you associate with being *on task.* Applying multiple frames or glasses to each picture often brings attention to relationships between separate features.

On the one hand, combining characteristics we noted about the body language in a photograph enables us to build our case. If we decide that a person seems to be on task, we find other features to support our original decision. When we relabel a photograph *on task* that we had initially labeled *off task,* we have to re-examine the feature that we wrote to prove that the person was off task. Thus if *standing* was a feature that initially signaled to us that the person was off task, we have to consider ways that standing could indicate that a person was on task when we change the title from *off task* to *on task.*

In short, we have to do what debaters do. We have to take the opposite position from our original one and re-assemble our evidence to support a point we have just argued against. But by switching characteristics, we can see that the evidence for one decision, like the original decision itself, may not accurately describe what is happening.

Either way, combining characteristics rather than noting only single characteristics in isolation is important. When we note that people we consider *off task* because they are not looking at a book may be because they are thinking about what they have just read, we realize that single cause-and-effect statements are limited. Another example is when we consider students *off task* because they talk from time to time, even though their words might be exploring the ideas they just read.

Cause-and-effect statements are limiting because they imply that what we do is one-dimensional rather than multidimensional. Thus, a remark such as "since they are off task, they are not learning," fails to indicate the possibility that features of being off task such as silence and talking are as important to note as the fact that the student is not looking at print. But looking at print is only one feature of the student's activity. In fact, using the single feature "looking at print" alone to determine whether a person is "on task" fails to show the complexity of what we do. It also fails to show the interrelationships among different characteristics. Consequently, it can become easier to see that changing just one characteristic—standing rather than sitting—is not really possible. Characteristics are interrelated and if one changes, others do. In observation we are not seeing a series of snapshots but an ongoing dynamic process.

THE USES AND LIMITS OF OUR FILTERS

Let me share with you a summary of an excerpt from *Tales of the Dervishes* by Idries Shah (1970):

> It seems that two garbage men had been shopping in the bazaar for some time. As they were about to leave the bazaar, they found themselves in the section where perfume was sold. Suddenly, one of the garbage men fell down and seemed to be breathing in a very irregular way. Many people came close to both the suffering garbage man and his partner to offer some help. But no sooner had people begun to come and offer various smelling salts as well as various types of herbs and perfume for the stricken man to smell, when his partner lifted him onto his back and carried him out of the perfume section of the bazaar.
>
> People followed to see whether they could still be of help and because they were curious. The garbage man took his partner to a section of the bazaar where garbage was collected and took what the perfume dealers considered to be the foulest smelling garbage and placed it beneath the nose of the stricken man. After a very short time, the man regained consciousness, to the astonishment of onlookers.

On one level this tale reminds us that one person's meat is another person's poison. More importantly, it reminds us of how ignorance about the background of a person we are looking at can prevent us from interacting appropriately with that person.

Activity 8

To highlight the fact that knowing something about a person can affect our perception, go back to the six pictures in Activity 6, and, after looking at the pictures again, write some questions you would like to ask about the people in the photographs.

Thinking about the Alternatives

Here are some questions others asked:

Are the students bright, medium, or not so bright?

Do the students have to take a test and are they in the process of preparing for it?

Are the students on a break at the time the pictures were taken?

Since I am seeing people who I cannot hear, I wonder whether those in the pictures are hearing impaired?

I can't see a central point of attention, so I wonder what the teacher had told the students to do?

One value of questions is that they often make explicit the types of glasses we are wearing, the types of frames we are putting around what we see. When we ask about the students' level, we are implying that how much people know in some continuum is of value. Whether the person is keen on learning more, regular in attendance, original in thinking, sincere, or truthful are not as central.

If, on the other hand, we ask how much schooling the students have had, we imply that previous schooling is an index of value in some way. If we were to ask whether the students had jobs, we would imply that work would be important for student development. Asking about students' ability to care for others would imply we valued charity in those we taught.

That we reveal our beliefs in the questions we ask about our students is not news, of course. What may be news is that the questions we ask, and thus the beliefs we consider vital, may not be seen as vital by either those we are asking about or others looking at the same students.

By comparing your questions with those of others and seeing that their questions may be as important as yours, you have an opportunity to reconsider the importance of your beliefs—and to see that your "glasses" present a limited view of reality. The limited view revealed by your questions may or may not be related to any true reality. Whether the garbage man in Shah's tale would have been revived by perfume or other scents over time rather than garbage we cannot tell from the story as it is. By carrying the panting garbage man to the garbage so quickly, his partner provided no chance to try experiencing a different reality.

If you are used to asking a lot of questions before observing, try observing without asking any questions. Look as if you are seeing for the first time, with no knowledge of who the people are, where they are, what they are doing, or what they are like. Characterize what you see in a range of ways first. Play with the data first, and then ask questions. In *Zorba the Greek*, Kazantzakis reveals the potential excitement possible from such a process (looking first, asking later):

> [Zorba] has been all over the racked and chaotic Balkans and observed everything with his little falcon-like eyes, which he constantly opens wide in amazement. Things we are accustomed to, and which we pass by indifferently, suddenly rise up in front of Zorba like fearful enigmas. Seeing a woman pass by, he stops in consternation.
>
> "What is that mystery?" he asks. "What is a woman, and why does she turn our heads? Just tell me, I ask you, what's the meaning of that?"
>
> He interrogates himself with the same amazement when he sees everything every day as if for the first time.
>
> (Kazantzakis, 1952, p. 51)

If you are keen on continuing to explore body language, as well as other communications without language, such as clothing and other adornment, invite some of your students to take photographs of class activities. Over time, have pictures taken of the same participants outside of class as well. Then, after a few weeks pass, have students sort the pictures in small groups on their own. Once in a while, ask to join the students as they discuss the pictures in order to introduce them to some of the activities in which you engaged in this section of this book. Their views of each other and of teachers and others can be as stable and one-dimensional as ours. Don Quixote was not meant to represent one Spanish man in the sixteenth century but all of us at all times. It will be exciting to see whether such joint exploration leads you and your students to the same amazement Zorba exhibited, a sense of surprise that led him to see "everything every day as if for the first time."

Optional Activity: Clothes As Body Language

In the appendix, Activity 8A under "Communications without Language," shows us ways our perceptions of clothes as part of body language affect how we deal with others.

FEEDBACK

*T*HE MANY MEANINGS OF "O.K."

"O.K." constitutes one of the most frequent comments after student responses in classes in the English-speaking world. The origin of "O.K." makes it an appropriate comment—"O.K." stands for "All Correct," spelled "Oll Korrect" in nineteenth-century America. If "All" was spelled with an O and "Correct" with a K in present-day classrooms, it is hard to imagine anyone saying "O.K." as a reaction. (Stacey, 1989, pp. 57, 58)

I often wonder how people reacted to statements before 1839—the first record of "O.K." in print—because if I did, I would use their expression. I have been saying "O.K." in class, as well as out, so frequently that I wonder if it means anything, let alone what its origin suggested it once meant.

Below are listed some dialogs containing "O.K." Below each dialog are written two paraphrases of "O.K."

1. Boy extremely interested in girl: Do you want to come over tomorrow?

    Girl not sure of her interest in boy: O.K.

   First meaning: Yes, I guess so.

   Second meaning: Yes, I'd really like to.

2. Wife to husband: I got the mail.

    Husband to wife: O.K.

   First meaning: I heard you.

   Second meaning: I'm busy and don't want to look at it now.

3. Teacher to student in hall in school: Take off your hat!

    Student in hall to teacher and peers: O.K.

   First meaning: If you say so.

   Second meaning: Yes, sir.

4. Teacher: How many elements are there in water?

    Student: Two?

    Teacher: O.K.

   First meaning: I heard you.

   Second meaning: I'm going to the next student.

5. Son to mother: I'm going out now, O.K.?

First meaning: Can I go?

Second meaning: What time should I be back?

Perhaps one of the reasons that "O.K." is used so frequently is that it can mean so many different things; often it has little to do with endorsing, or approving, or indicating correctness. It may simply close a conversation, indicating we are not sure what to say.

Activity 1

Tape your class, or a colleague's. Listen to the tape, and on the blank lines below, transcribe two or three exchanges in which someone says "O.K." Then, on the broken lines, write two possible meanings of O.K. in the exchanges you transcribed. (Note that if you are working in a language other than English, you will find "O.K." widely used; also, other languages have words with a similar function, such as *vale, d'accord, zain*.)

1. Person A: _____
   _____
   _____

   Person B: _____
   _____
   _____

   First meaning: _
   Second meaning: _

2. Person A: _____
   _____
   _____

   Person B: _____
   _____
   _____

   First meaning: _
   Second meaning: _

3. Person A: _____
   _____
   _____

Feedback

Person B:
_____
_____
_____

First meaning: _
Second meaning: _

Thinking about the Alternatives

After teachers listen to tapes of their teaching and hear many instances of "O.K.," I have frequently heard them express awareness of an overuse of O.K.: "I'm going to try to stop saying it so much." In discussing changing the way to play tennis, Gallwey had this to say: "It is much more difficult to break a habit where there is no adequate replacement for it. There is no need to fight old habits." (Gallwey, 1974, pp. 77, 79) Substituting other comments is likely to reduce the frequency of "O.K." One source of substitutions for "O.K." would be other comments made during a class. As you listened for instances of "O.K.," you probably could not have helped but hear many other types of comments after student responses, both those considered acceptable and those that contained errors.

After the student response below write as many substitutions for "O.K.," to signify an acceptable response as you and your partner recall hearing while you listened for instances of "O.K." on your tapes. Then discuss with your partner still other possible alternatives for O.K.

TEACHER: What are some ways we can personally conserve water?

STUDENT: We can turn off the water when we brush our teeth. I ask my parents to do this, too. And I ask my father to turn off the faucet when he shaves as well. If we all save 1 or 2 gallons a day, millions are saved.

Substitutions for "O.K." we heard
_____
_____
_____

Substitutions for "O.K." we dreamt up
_____
_____
_____

The most frequent comment that many hear in place of "O.K." is "very good." Some have heard "thank you." Calling on another student with "Who else would like to answer?" or the mention of a student's name was also heard.

Here are some comments others dreamt up:

"I hate to turn it off, but I think I should; I'm glad you do."

"Interesting."

"Really?"

"Is that for real, or is it from a campaign?"

"You should do an ad for saving water on TV."

If you want to substitute some other comments for "O.K." in your own teaching, write a few substitutions either in your lesson plan or on the blackboard before the lesson. If you have a few instances of feedback readily available, you can look in your lesson plan or on the board and select one that fits the response, and then say it to the participating student. Over time, see what a wider range of comments sound like on the tape. And see how you and a few students you ask seem to feel about the variety of comments substituted for "O.K."

FEEDBACK WITHOUT SPOKEN LANGUAGE

My emphasis so far on listening to the audiotape and dealing with "O.K." orally obscures the fact that much feedback is provided without spoken words, or along with spoken words.

Activity 2

On the blank lines at the end of the exchange below, write down some ways you would provide feedback without speaking.

TEACHER: [Standing next to student during an in-class writing assignment and reading over the student's shoulder.] Let me read the letter you are writing.

STUDENT'S LETTER:

Dear Granpa,
 We're gonna call you next week. I am in school now. My teacher told the class to rite to a person they love. She helps us spell words we cannot remember. I hope the dogs do not mis us to much. We mis you and the dogs.

Thinking about the Alternatives

While most of us seem to feel it our duty to add a *d* to Granpa, and the *w* to *r* in *rite* and an *s* to each *mis*, by concentrating on the meaning of the lines, some alternatives are possible. One teacher wrote, "I'd like to get a letter like this." Another wrote, "Your spelling was clever, and I understood it perfectly. I'm sure your grandfather would also. Next time you write to your grandpa, add the letters that I am adding to these words on this piece of scrap paper—add a 'd' to 'Granpa,' add the 'w' to 'r' in 'write,' and add an 's' to each 'mis'." One teacher put a P.S. on the letter: "I am very proud of your granddaughter.—Mrs. Blodget, teacher." Another teacher underlined the words that had been misspelled and wrote "Be careful—watch your spelling." All these comments except the last were written with blue or black ink; the last was written in red.

One teacher put a sticker saying "Great" on the sheet of paper. Another wrote nothing, simply putting her hand on the child's shoulder as she read the letter. One shook the child's hand and smiled after reading the letter.

If your students write, see what kinds of comments you have written in their books. See what color pens you have been using. Look at what your colleague does as well. Think back on comments others have written on your work. Try providing some feedback you have not recently given, even if it just means changing the color of the pen. These techniques work also if student writing is on blackboards.

With forty students in a class, of course, detailed comments take a great deal of time so some teachers select examples of students' work from each class to provide feedback on. Then they ask the students who have received feedback that day to read the writing of other students and write feedback on it. Peer conferences thus provide a chance for students to experience different types of feedback.

If we want to alter our proportion of "O.K." as feedback, we have a wide range of mediums, including not only written words but also intonation and pictures, to name two others.

THE MULTIPLE CHARACTERISTICS OF FEEDBACK

Sketches, written comments, "O.K." spoken during class, and a few substitutions for "O.K." have all, I hope, focused some attention on feedback. But the fact that instances of feedback, like any other communications, have multiple characteristics has not been noted. As a reminder that communications have many facets, I have provided some instances of feedback in a range of ways. The instances of feedback we will use were provided after a student error, with the expectation that the student would try to respond again correctly after the intervening feedback.

I collected these instances from tapes of ten teachers teaching the same bit of language, and I used videotape because as I have observed feedback, I have noticed that much feedback is given without language.

Activity 3

On your own, group the instances of feedback that follow the teacher-student exchange, below. Group on the basis of as many characteristics as you can, or want to, in the pairs of columns provided. It's "O.K." to put some instances under both columns, or some in neither, since in most groupings, black-and-white, clear-cut decisions are not always possible. As you put instances of feedback under the pairs of columns—the T's—write words describing the characteristics on the line forming the top of the T.

These instances of feedback, like "O.K.," and most other communications, can have more than one meaning. Consequently, as always, your groupings cannot be wrong. I do not expect that you will group the instances of feedback as either I or others have.

TEACHER: [Holding up a toy pair of boxing gloves] "What am I holding?"
STUDENT: "Boxing glove."

Feedback possibilites:

1. O.K. Very good,
2. Boxing glove? [said with rising intonation]
3. [Writes *boxing glove* on the blackboard and draws a green line under the words and a blank after *e*] Ninety-nine percent correct!
4. [Writes *glove* on the blackboard with white chalk and circles the *e* with red chalk]
5. You identified the object. Your pronunciation, though . . .
6. [Waits until the student says the answer again—says nothing and does nothing]
7. [Shakes head sideways]
8. Who knows the right answer?
9. [Writes these letters and spaces on the blackboard: b o x i n _ g l o v e _]
10. [Holds up a picture of a bumblebee]
11. Yes—but just toy ones.
12. [Writes a *z* on the blackboard]
13. [Holds pair of gloves closer to student's face]
14. Wrong.
15. Right words. Wrong grammar. Make *glove* plural.
16. Boxing glovezzzz. [Stressing final sound]
17. [Arches eyebrows in mock surprise]
18. [Writes *boxing glove* on the blackboard and draws three lines under *e* with great energy]
19. Another student shouts "Gloves!"
20. Strange thing for me to be holding, huh?
21. [Holds up two fingers of right hand]

Feedback ■ 77

78 ■ Applications of Observing

Thinking about the Alternatives

Below are some ways others have grouped the twenty-one instances of feedback, together with the labels or descriptions of the characteristics. Don't feel you have to work your way through all of these, but study a few. And as you compare your groupings, read the comments.

The real point of these groupings is not to prove that some items belong in one column rather than another. Rather, the groupings force us to ask questions about what we are doing and saying. Terms we use on a regular basis, when applied to actual instances, do not have as clear-cut meanings as they seem to.

As we look and listen and group what we see and hear, we may become aware that our beliefs about what is important in our practices may keep us from seeing what we are actually doing. And when we look at the meaning of our communications, we may see that they are different from what we had thought they were before we looked.

Words alone	Nonwords or words plus others
1, 5, 8, 11, 14, 15, 20	

Negative or positive	Informative
1, 2, 3, 7, 8, 13, 14, 15, 16, 17, 18, 19	3, 9, 10, 11, 12, 16, 18, 19, 20, 21

Whether any instances contained *words alone* is hard to determine without listening to the tape together. The transcript indicates intonation or features of speaking other than words only in 2, 16, and 19. If "O.K. Very good" were said sarcastically, then it would qualify for the second column of the first T. This can be said for any of those listed under *words alone* and reminds us of the many meanings of *O.K.*, depending not on the sounds themselves but on the accompanying tone of voice, intonation, and stress.

Feedback ■ 79

As you have noticed, some items are listed under both headings in the second T. Is saying that something is 99 percent correct (3) positive, or informative, or both? Does a green line (3) indicate something positive if one is used to red lines indicating something negative? While underlining the e might locate the place to concentrate on in altering the response, are three lines necessary? (18) And is energy necessary? Does energy move beyond information?

No doubt you and your partner are engaging in the same types of questioning with the characteristics you each noticed. If you are not, try to do so, because the grouping of communications into neat black-and-white categories is not really an easy task nor perhaps even a possible or desirable task. But the attempt often reveals facets of communications not previously noticed, which is a central goal of having contrasting conversations.

Shows teacher is in charge	Does not show anyone in charge
1–18, 20, 21	19

Specifies error	Does not specify error
3, 4, 5, 9, 12, 15, 18, 21	1, 2, 6, 7, 8, 10, 11, 13, 14, 16, 17, 19, 20

Some, after discussing feedback, contend that its only purpose is to keep control, and thus it does not matter what type of feedback is provided since its function, like the function of "O.K." on a TV talk show, is to remind people who is the master of ceremonies.

Even when the teacher is exerting a lot of energy to specify the error, which seems the case in 16, with the stress on the final sound, one wonders whether anyone is noticing, or hearing, or listening. Consequently, 16 was placed under *does not specify error* even though the intention of the stressing is, no doubt, to specify the error, or at least its location. Does the intonation in 2 specify an error? Well, it does in regular conversation. The problem is that the intonation could mean "It's not boxing gloves but work gloves," rather than "It's not glove but gloves." Intonation indicates an error but not whether it is semantic, grammatical, or in fact any other type.

When the student shouts the correct word in 19, one could argue that the error is specified, but in fact giving the answer may not indicate anything to a person who may be unaware of what was said in the first place. In fact, the issue of whether the person who makes the error is aware of any of the attempts to specify it is not easy to settle. Consequently, those who noticed the characteristic *specifies* error kept changing the instances of feedback they thought fit under that category.

Implicit information	Explicit information
2, 3, 4, 9, 12, 16, 18	5, 7, 14, 15, 21

Discouraging	Encouraging
2, 13, 18, ?	11, 20, ?

Is the word *pronunciation* in 5 more explicit than the green line in 3 and the red circle in 4? Do we need language to be explicit? Why is the stress in 16 not explicit information? It locates the error. The shaking head in 7 and the *wrong* in 14 are explicit—the fact that an error has been made is indicated. But nothing about the nature of the error is indicated, so it might be argued that they are less explicit than the two fingers used as a symbol of plural in 21.

The *discouraging/encouraging* pair needs so much discussion that as you can see I have put question marks in both columns. By matching instances with the labels we use, we see more clearly that there are many facets to any communication. And we see that the labels we use so easily in the usual conversations have less precise meanings than we think.

Appeal to the eye	Appeal to other senses
3, 4, 7, 9, 10, 12, 13, 17, 18, 21	1, 2, 3, 5, 8, 11, 14, 16, 19, 20

Emotional	Unemotional
13, 16, 17, 18, 19, 20	1, 2, 3, 5, 6, 7, 8, 9, 11, 11, 14, 15

While the instances that appeal to the eye seem the most clear-cut, if no one is looking, they cannot appeal to the eyes! Whereas we may agree that some communications are available for the eyes of the students, whether they are looking or not we can determine only from observation. Even then, they may be looking but not seeing.

In fact, any of the twenty-one items could be emotional or unemotional, depending on how the items were communicated. As you saw in Activity 1, "O.K." can mean a wide range of things, depending on the relationship between the characters, the setting, and the purposes each has. Therefore "Boxing glove?" in 2 can be said to mean, "Do you mean to use the singular?" Or it can mean, "How can you be so stupid as to use the wrong word?"—to name two possibilities.

Optional Activity: Applying Others' Characteristics

Activity 3A under Feedback in the appendix provides an opportunity to explore the characteristics of feedback that others have identified.

TRYING OUT ALTERNATIVE FEEDBACK

"If you give positive feedback, they will learn more; encourage them; be explicit; just give information, don't get emotional and upset." So go some of the cliches about giving feedback. When we try to match some actual communications with the advice we hear, we realize like Weiner, who pioneered in the field of cybernetics (the study of automatic control in mechanical, electrical, and human systems) that the general comments made in the usual conversations say little: "the more probable the message, the less information it gives. Cliches, for example, are less illuminating than great poems." (Weiner, 1967, p. 31)

Understanding the Dimensions

The usual comments are not only general, but also one-dimensional. When we grouped the instances of feedback in Activity 3, we saw that most instances of feedback had many characteristics. For example, in 2, "Boxing glove?" (said with rising intonation) has these characteristics: (1) shows the teacher in charge; (2) does not specify the error; (3) is implicit; (4) appeals to other senses: the modulation of the voice is reflected by intonation and has to be heard since it cannot be seen by the eyes; (5) is unemotional.

Select two or three out of the twenty-one instances of feedback from this section (page 77) and think about the characteristics of those that especially interest you. If you need help citing characteristics, refer back to the groupings you and others did in Activity 3.

After noting at least three characteristics of each instance of feedback that intrigued you, using labels you or others generated, you will see more clearly that discussing feedback in one-dimensional terms usually fails to describe some of the variables that may be affecting the feedback we are providing.

Generating Alternatives

Now you are ready to generate alternative types of feedback. As you do, focus first on altering one feature of one instance of feedback that you have used in your teaching. If few of your existing instances of feedback are emotional, make them emotional by getting some examples from the instances under the category *emotional* (use the characteristics you and your colleague discovered in Activity 3).

Play with the instances. Say "Boxing glove?" not only with rising intonation but as if you could not imagine anyone saying such a thing. Be emotional if you normally are not. If you are, make a comment as if you are practicing being neutral in your speech so that no emotion can be detected.

In short, do the opposite. The employment of opposites enables you to vary what you do so that you have an opportunity to see more clearly what you are doing. And as the German educator Froebel, who, among other achievements, is known as the founder of the kindergarten, pointed out in a discussion of multiple points of view:

> The teacher, by employing the method of opposites, attempts to convey to the student the complexity of life situations—to describe them as completely as possible. The use of opposites by the teacher prevents the pupil from resting too quickly in any result or becoming too easily satisfied with himself.
>
> (Froebel, quoted in Broudy, 1965, p. 122)

Naturally you will start with those characteristics you consider most important. After you use them, begin to note ways that the features you consider important are not important at all. For example, you might consider being emotional important. After noting many instances where you were emotional in treating errors, getting genuinely annoyed at the same errors over and over, substitute a comment made in a neutral tone of voice, or write words such as "try again" on the blackboard. Then, having substituted some unemotional feedback for emotional feedback, note some reasons why being emotional is not necessarily important at all.

If you think explicit information is important, stop giving it. In fact, doing nothing except waiting provides an opportunity to see to what extent other types of treatments are needed. When waiting enables learners to repair what they have said on their own, it means our notions of feedback may need to be reconsidered.

From time to time, observe another teacher or watch or listen to a tape of yourself with another person. Or watch a television program. Write down a half dozen instances of different types of feedback.

*D*OES OUR FEEDBACK REFLECT OUR BELIEFS?

By comparing feedback we use with advice that others give and that we believe in, we can compare our practices with our beliefs. Frank Smith, who relates information processing to reading, gives some advice on providing feedback in teaching reading. If students are taught to ask "What does this sentence mean?" rather than simply "Have I said the words correctly?," the text itself can provide its own feedback. In fact, providing immediate knowledge of results by stating the words they misread can be distracting because such feedback emphasizes the pronuncation of individual words rather than the meaning of words joined together. (Smith, 1975, pp. 234, 235)

Activity 4

Below is an example of student reading.

> A CAPTION IN A BOOK IS AS FOLLOWS: This stamp is more expensive than the other one. It costs 15 cents.
>
> A STUDENT'S ORAL READING OF THE CAPTION IS: This stamp is more expensive the other one. It costs 15 cent.

An omission occurs as well as the rendering of the word "cent" in the wrong form. Below are some examples of attention to the errors. On the broken lines next to each example of attention, write *c* for congruent if you think the type of attention given is congruent with Smith's advice that the text itself can provide its own feedback. Saying the word that the student misread would be an example of feedback that would be incongruent with Smith's advice, for example. For now, ignore the long blank line under each demonstration of attention to the errors.

1. Who can read it right? Come on, someone else! ___
   _____

2. Just look at the sentences again. Then, turn and look at me and say what you remember—I'm only interested in the meaning. [Seems to be said in a way that reflects patience and interest]
   ___
   _____

3. Than, than, than and plural—come on, pay attention! ___
   _____

4. I can't believe this. ___
   _____

5. [Draws a line under *than* and under the *s* in *costs*.] ___
   _____

6. Say the meaning in your own words. ___
   _____

7a. Look at the board and tell me if I am saying the words on the board right. ___
    _____

  b. This stamp is more expensive the other one. Right? Wrong? ___
     _____

  c. [Student says: You left out *than*—more expensive *than*.] ___
     _____

  d. It costs 15 cent. The other one costs only 3 cent. ___
     _____

  e. [Another student says: Plural, plural!] ___
     _____

84 ■ Applications of Observing

> 8a. I'd like each of you to write the sentences as you heard them said just now. ---
>
> b. Then, compare what you write with the board and make any changes necessary so that they are the same. ---
>
> 9. How many stamps are in the picture? ---
>
> 10. Underline the words that show a comparison is being made. ---
>
> 11. Write down the letter on the stamps that is at the end of the words between the numbers. [The only word between the numbers 15 and 3 is the word *cents*. Just as the word *cents* appears between numbers on some of the stamps reproduced in the back of this book.] ---

Since Frank Smith implies that the material itself should provide the information for a learner to use, he might not write a *c* on any of the broken lines. But another way to consider congruence is to determine whether a particular communication is close to or far from the advice given. Looking at congruence in this way, I put a *c* next to 2, 5, 6, 7, 8, 10, and 11. In each of these, the teacher in some way seems to be attempting to draw the attention of the students back to the text to find differences between what is in the text and what was said in the oral reading—between print and speech. The words are said, but the intention of the spoken words seems to be to get the students to attend to the printed words.

Activity 5

Go back to the eleven instances of feedback that you just examined for their congruence with Smith's advice and on the long blank lines rewrite some of them. To rewrite them, we first have to note the characteristics from your groupings, or those of others. Then take one or two of the contrasting characteristics in the groupings as listed in Activity 3—emotional/unemotional—and translate them into a different instance of feedback.

These steps can be illustrated with item 1 in Activity 4. To change "Who can read it right? Come on, someone else!" from *words plus tone of voice* to *words only*, the question and comment could be written on the blackboard, minus the exclamation mark. By doing this, it would become *unemotional* rather than *emotional*. And, it might also no longer fit under the category *discouraging*. Or, if it did, it would seem to be less discourag-

Feedback ■ 85

ing anyway. Alternatively, the lines could be said humorously, with a smile, rather than what seems to be impatiently. The feedback would still have the feature *words plus*, but the feature *discouraging* might not now apply.

Or, if you consider 7c an instance of *teacher not in charge* because a student says "you left out *than*—more expensive *than*," then you can generate parallel instances of student feedback by teaching students to ask for feedback about their performance. They can be taught to turn a typical teacher comment such as "you aren't saying the words right" into a question: "Tell me, am I saying the words right?"

This change from statement to question changes the source of the feedback about word form from the teacher to the student or to another student. After all, the question "Am I saying the words right?" can be directed to either the teacher or a fellow student. But either way, the communication can now be placed under the column *teacher in charge*.

If one of your pairs of characteristics was *gave answer/gave partial answer* or *clue*, then the *than* in item 3 can be replaced by "add a word that we use in comparisons" or "add a word that rhymes with 'ran.'" Both of these provide partial information, which some might call *clues*. *Plural* can be replaced with *costs*, since plural is a clue rather than an answer, if we consider stating the word needed as meaning *gave answer*.

If one of your pairs of characteristics was *taking people's tongue away/allowing people to use their tongue* or *teaching people to be shy/ teaching that we don't have to use perfect form as we learn*—variations of *discouraging/encouraging*—and you thought 1, 2, and 4 fit the first of each pair—the left column—then you could select an instance from the right-hand column of the same pair. Using an instance of feedback in your teaching that you collected in your observation rather than writing a new one is a reminder of the close link between observing and teaching. In place of "Pay attention," simply try in your teaching one of the instances that you placed in the right-hand column of these same pairs as a result of your observation.

Rewriting and trying one of two alternative characteristics of feedback each week in your teaching will provide a great range of instances different from those observed. If you rewrite and try out more than one or two you will have so much new information that it will not be possible to observe how different instances of feedback affect student responses. Additionally, too many changes in our teaching all at once can be disconcerting to students, as well as to our own stability.

FEEDBACK AS A CIRCLE

Dealing with the form/dealing with the meaning or content are features that many come up with as they play with feedback in their observations. Like many features, *dealing with the meaning* is an alternative type of feedback that can be dealt with as we teach before the task is performed, as well as after. In instance 2, in Activity 5, ". . . I'm only interested in the meaning" and in instance 6, "Say the meaning in your own words," we have features we can group under *dealing with the meaning*. In Activity 3, item 11, "Yes but just toy ones," and item 20, "Strange thing for me to be holding, huh?," also deal with meaning.

Providing these types of comments before we set a task in our classroom is an alternative to rewriting feedback to use in our classes after tasks are performed. Thus, before a reading task, you may say something such as "We are interested in meaning—that's why I want you all to look at the sentence, read it silently, and then turn to me. And when I call on you, say, in your own words, what meaning the words express." One meaning of feedback, after all, is to feed back information to a source so that the original source will adjust its signal.

Seeing feedback as a circle means that information about results can begin a second cycle as well as come after a first cycle. Instances of feedback can consequently become added information given when setting tasks rather than simply information given after the performance of tasks.

With a partner, take some of the instances of feedback you have already used or rewritten as a result of your observation and analysis of feedback. Incorporate some of the instances in the words you use in your class to set one or two tasks as well as in the information you supply after the tasks have been completed, O.K.? For example, if you are used to correcting a student's grammar after a student speaks, consider writing the words *singular* and *plural* on the blackboard with words that fit under each. Then have the students look at the board for a few minutes before you start questioning.

*T*URNING FEEDBACK UPSIDE DOWN

A neighborhood organizer named Saul Alinksy, in discussing the need to see another person's point of view, wrote, "[the] grasp of the duality of all phenomena is vital in our understanding of politics. It frees one from the myth that one approach is positive and another negative. There is no such thing in life. One [person's] positive is another [person's] negative." (Alinsky, 1971, p. 18) The proverb "One person's meat is another person's poison" reminds us of the same point.

In analyzing ways different instances of feedback affect student responses, as well as other communications we make, we are limited by our own beliefs of what is good and bad. One way to move beyond this limitation in our analysis of what we observe is to label as "bad" those instances of feedback we consider "good," and then write down at least one way such bad feedback can be good.

Of course, in a way it is a real test for a person who believes that one should be supportive and explicit and use visual information to see how "Who can read it right? Come on, someone else!" can be positive. But what if we think a student is not trying his best in our class? What if we think a group of students are just not engaged? Might a few moments in our class used for a sharing of genuine emotions, which express the need for students to do more to reach their expectations, be positive? What if we think that there is no need to draw a line—visual information in addition to words—or be explicit by saying "you forgot the plural on *cents*"—because the students had earlier read the sentences correctly and thus seem not to need explicit information but the proverbial "kick in the pants"?

As you continue to play with feedback in your teaching and observing as well as other teaching practices, once in a while write down a judgment you make. Write some reasons for your judgment. Then write the opposite judgment and write some reasons for it as a way to see from a different perspective.

Such a different perspective may in fact be just the way a student may be seeing the practice. Children's views of spankings or a lot of praise are, after all, often the opposite of their parents'. Such opposite judgments are likely from students to teachers as well as from children to parents. But since students may not reveal their opposite views explicitly, we can generate them by giving arguments in class to support as good our judgments of something we consider bad, and vice versa.

We turn now to the point made in the Introduction, turning our beliefs upside down and inside out in our observation and analysis of our teaching can free us to try things in our teaching that otherwise we would feel reluctant to try. For example, one teacher considered it bad to say no after incorrect student responses. "Students will get discouraged; students will think I am critical" are arguments used to support the use of *no* as bad. After being told to write two advantages of saying no, the teacher wrote "students might try harder since they will see that you have high expectations and the 'no' will make your expectations clearer." The teacher also wrote that saying no might be more honest than simply saying "try again," since the reason for trying again is that the first try is wrong.

In your teaching, observation, and analysis, try turning things inside out and upside down with your judgments and beliefs as one additional way of substituting alternatives for "O.K." . . . O.K.?

PATTERNS IN CLASSROOM TALK

CREATING SPACE FOR EXPLORATORY TALK

Douglas Barnes, a professor at Leeds University in England, analyzed speech used by pupils during group work in English, science, and history classrooms. According to Barnes, teachers' questions and comments affect the degree to which language spoken by students is *exploratory talk* or *final draft talk*. (Barnes, 1976, p. 108)

In the classes Barnes described and analyzed, as well as in those he knew about through reports from others, Barnes put forward the suggestion that pupils rarely are asked to state their own views. And even when they are, the teachers often treat the pupils' responses the same way they treat other responses—with a comment such as "Very good."

In discussing the role of exploratory talk in juxtaposition to final draft talk, he proposes this explanation for lack of responses from pupils:

> When teachers complain about classes who will not talk they often present this as a moral failing in the pupils; it is more likely that the pupils have learnt from their schooling that their knowledge is irrelevant in a context determined by teachers, examinations, school syllabuses, and so on.
>
> (Barnes, 1976, p. 127)

Activity 1

With a colleague, if possible, or alone, write an x for exploratory talk next to the questions below that you (both) agree have the potential for allowing pupils to respond with some understanding rather than by rote, to say something they might not have said before in exactly the same way, to pause, to rephrase—to explore rather than produce a pat answer.

1. If you divide 20 centimeters by 10, what do you get?   ___
2. What color is the Atlantic Ocean on the map?   X
3. I want each of you to measure one object that is small—that you can pick up—and one that is big—that you cannot pick up. Use these meter sticks and write the name of the object and then the dimensions you find. Do your measuring in the usual pairs.   X
4. O.K., now look at this ball in my hand. This ball—an example of a physical property or a chemical property? Remember the definition we went over yesterday.   X
5. What's a furnace? (Asked by one pupil of fellow classmates)   X
6. Who can say the lines of the dialog—word for word?   ___

> 7. Peter is angry—he has just been told that his father will not allow him to go on the school trip because he thinks he might not be watched carefully enough. Write some words that reflect some of Peter's feelings. _X_
>
> 8. Now that you have finished reading the passage, answer these questions I have written on the board:
>
>   a. Who wrote the story? ---
>
>   b. Who caught the boy stealing the toothpaste? ---
>
>   c. How did you feel about the boy's stealing? _X_
>
> 9. What feelings do you have about the boy who took the toothpaste in the story? _X_

Thinking about Responses

The items that are most frequently marked x the first time through are 5, 7, 8c, and 9. In fact, all the other items produced responses of a few words that were followed by an "O.K." or a "Very good," suggesting that those asking the questions were interested in finding out whether learners had remembered something.

Item 5, "What's a furnace?"—an example of the classic "What's this?"—produced a great deal of talk. Usually, this question produces only a word or two. But in 5, the question was asked by a learner who did not know what a furnace was, and he asked his classmates rather than the teacher. The teacher did not contribute to the conversation. The excerpt below contains a part of the response to the learner's exploration:

> 1. It's the ... uh ... machine that blow hot air.
>
> 2. Hot air? No, the air conditioner?
>
> 3. No, the hot air, around the house.
>
> 4. The boiler. Is called the boiler.
>
> 5. I have a furnace downstairs.
>
> 6. Maybe there's both the boiler and ... uh ... the furnace?
>
> 7. ... boiling water on the stove ...

The hesitations (1 and 7), the disagreement (3), questioning (2 and 6) are some characteristics of exploratory talk. In the exchange about the furnace, from which the seven lines are excerpted, those trying to produce their own knowledge—to develop the meaning from negotiation and reference to their own experiences—spoke seven lines and about forty words. As the conversation above was ending, the teacher said only: "Maybe 'boiler' is the British term." And this comment seems more like a learner comment—a contribution of information to develop meaning—rather than a rating or an evaluation of a learner comment.

EXPLORATORY TALK OR FINAL DRAFT TALK—DOING A FLIP-FLOP

Activity 2

Below are the nine tasks from the preceding excerpt with some additional blank lines under each. On these lines, for any task you marked with an x, rewrite the questions so that they would be more likely to elicit shorter responses that require the restatement of information or the production of pat answers.

On the blank lines under the tasks you did not mark with an x, rewrite the questions so they are likely to lead to longer responses, which would have learners exploring and producing their own knowledge rather than restating information. Under item 1 is a question another person wrote; this is an example of a rewritten question.

(Margin note: You didn't follow the directions. (Maybe, however, you got more out of the exercise doing it your way.))

1. If you divide 20 centimeters by 10, what do you get?
   If 20 centimeters divided by 10 centimeters is 2, how much is 20 cents divided by 10 cents, 200 yen divided by 100 yen, and how many 20-franc stamps could you buy if you have 200 francs?

2. What color is the Atlantic Ocean on the map?
   What color is the Atlantic Ocean on the map—sky blue, navy blue or plain blue?

3. I want each of you to measure one object that is small—that you can pick up—and one that is big—that you cannot pick up. Use these meter sticks and write the name of the object and then the dimensions you find. Do your measuring in the usual pairs.
   You will measure two objects. Measure only height and length.

4. O.K., now look at this ball in my hand. This ball—an example of a physical property or a chemical property? Remember the definition we went over yesterday.
   Look at this ball. Can you name 3 three physical properties of it?

5. What's a furnace? (Asked by one pupil of fellow classmates)
   What is one function of a furnace?

6. Who can say the lines of the dialog—word for word?
   Who can say the dialog by interpreting it and assigning it your own meaning and feeling?

Patterns in Classroom Talk ■ 91

> 7. Peter is angry—he has just been told that his father will not allow him to go on the school trip because he thinks he might not be watched carefully enough. Write some words that reflect some of Peter's feelings.
>
> ✓ *Do you think that Peter felt his father was being unfair?*
>
> 8. Now that you have finished reading the passage, answer these questions I have written on the board:
>   a. Who wrote the story?
>   b. Who caught the boy stealing the toothpaste?
>   c. How did you feel about the boy's stealing?
>
> ✓ *a. What do you think the author's purpose was for writing this passage?*
> *b. How did the boy get caught stealing the toothpaste?*
> *c. Name one feeling you have about the boy stealing.*
>
> 9. What feelings do you have about the boy who took the toothpaste in the story?
>
> ✓ *Are you disappointed that the boy stole the toothpaste?*

Thinking about the Alternatives to Final Draft Talk

Item 1: The rewritten question was provided above. While there are still right answers—no room for speculation—there is the need for comparing. Since there are really five separate calculations, it is likely that those working on the question would be given the chance to use paper and pencil. This alone would alter the process and allow if nothing else a bit more time for the learners to deal with the question.

Item 2: Rather than limit the question about the globe to one color at a time, one teacher asked individual learners or pairs to write down at least five colors they see on the globe and then write down what each thinks a particular color represents. Again, comparisons are then necessary, and if the teacher allows responses that show thinking—being serious about the use of the word *thinks*—learners may explore more. The "blue" one learner might blurt out "stands for cold" as the oceans and lakes are noticed. Since water, even in tropical places, is often cool, such a response would not only represent exploratory talk but would remind all those listening that in fact colors on maps as in other places can have many meanings in addition to those intended. An understanding of the color scheme on the globe might be richer than insisting that each color had only one meaning.

Item 6: Rather than having students say dialogs "word for word," the teacher can ask students to substitute words. In place of "fine" in the classic "How are you?" dialog, a learner can share a genuine feeling—a few words, with a sketch next to each to illustrate meaning, can be on the blackboard as a cue. The learner can then be asked to use a word cued by a sketch so that the words in the lines have to be altered on command, requiring more than memory and rote for a quick substitution. The words can be said as they are, or learners can be asked to say the words as if they are tired, or sick, or full of energy, or uninterested, requiring the exploration of the use of intonation, pauses, and various facial expressions.

Item 8a: If we are interested in the name of an author, there is even less room for speculation than there is in doing sums. But we might be curious about the age of an author, when a particular work was written, the background, the place where the author lived. What statements in the story suggest the age of the author, the background, etcetera? So, rather than "Who wrote blank?" we may ask "When blank wrote blank, how old do you think blank was? Where did blank live? Do you think blank was rich? Had a family?" The options are great and each requires some connection between the lines from a story and the person as an author rather than simply the restatement of an author's name.

Item 8b: If learners are asked to make up questions to test their peers, they may need to explore more than if they are asked questions made by a teacher. Of course, when one learner responds to another, one will be back in the role of learner and one in the role of teacher. But often when peers ask each other they argue about the response—"I thought you asked when did the detective catch the boy, not who caught the boy." The furnace dialog shows some arguing, for example.

There is one way to alter the items: Write the questions on one side of note cards, with the answers on the other side. Then pass the cards out to those who did not know the answers, and they can ask others for the answers. When the answers are given, both can compare the answers with the ones on the backs of the note cards. But since the answers are set, the type of exploration that took place in the furnace exchange is less likely, even though in both cases learners are asking questions to which they don't know the answer.

While all of these alternatives still limit the range of responses, they do allow the learner to contribute something from experience. Or, as Barnes writes, they have the potential for allowing the learner to take responsibility for the adequacy of the response rather than looking "towards external criteria and distant, unknown audience." (Barnes, 1976, p. 113)

Of course, even the questions that have the potential to produce exploratory talk can turn into final draft talk. This can happen by treating responses that are not known beforehand as right or wrong. Exploratory talk can be transformed into final draft talk by teacher feedback such as "Very good" or "No, not what I wanted." Note that it does not matter if the comment by the teacher after the response is positive or negative. As Simon and Boyer say, "Positive and negative evaluations are not seen as opposites; they serve, in fact, exactly the same function—that of judging . . ." (Simon & Boyer, 1967, p. 16)

Activity 3

With a colleague, select questions from a textbook one of you is using. Then take one or two questions that require exploratory talk and alter them so that they require final draft talk. Take one or two questions that require final draft talk and alter them so that they require exploratory talk. Try asking the questions in both ways in your classes. Tape record the lessons.

Here are some examples:

1. TEXT: John plays on weekends.

   QUESTION LEADING TO FINAL DRAFT TALK: What does John do on weekends?

   QUESTIONS LEADING TO EXPLORATORY TALK: John is around 12; when he plays on weekends, what do you think he plays? What do you play on weekends? When I was 12, I played chess a lot, but most of my friends played baseball.

2. TEXT: (A picture showing two sketched faces; a dialog between two people printed below the sketches)

   QUESTION LEADING TO FINAL DRAFT TALK: How many faces are there?

   QUESTIONS LEADING TO EXPLORATORY TALK: Draw some lines on the sketches to show emotions the characters might be feeling, given what they are saying to each other.

The question to direct students to draw reminds us that the word *talk* in exploratory talk and final draft talk can be understood as a metaphor for thinking. Whether we have students drawing, acting, making models, producing sound effects, editing film, or writing essays, we can produce questions to lead them to explore or to get right answers.

Activity 4

Listen to a few minutes of the audio recording you made in Activity 3, in which you and a colleague altered some questions in a textbook to try in either of your classes. Write down a few examples of the questions you altered and the responses each produced.

_____
_____
_____
_____

Now change those questions that you altered that seemed to lead to long responses and hesitations and the construction of knowledge on the part of learners *back* into questions that you think will produce pat responses. And change those questions that seemed to lead to pat responses back to some that would more likely lead to exploration. In short, analyze and play with the two types of questions to see more and more characteristics of each type and the responses that each tends to produce.

_____
_____
_____

Initially, you might find, for example, that yes/no questions that you turned into question-word questions in order to elicit more language actually elicited less language. Turning the question-word questions back into yes/no questions may reveal that though the initial response to a yes/no question is just one word—yes or no—when students are given time, they quite often expand their response. Such expansion seems particularly common when the response is no. We seem to feel the need to explain or justify no responses.

You may find as well that the yes/no questions that ask students personal questions lead to cut-and-dried responses, while question-word questions about students' feelings produce tentative but long responses. By playing with the questions, we thus are likely to see both the effect of different characteristics of the same type of question and different effects of different questions.

You may even want to take some questions from examinations or standardized tests so you can compare the types of talk that different items tend to produce.

ALTERING THE PROPORTION OF QUESTION TYPES

You can support your goal for a lesson by altering the proportion of the types of questions you ask. If you want to remind pupils of the need to be able to respond to questions on certain types of examinations, ask a lot of questions that lead to final draft talk. If you want to see how pupils can use some language or new information in saying something they have not said before, ask some questions that lead to exploratory talk.

If you are not sure of your goals or intentions but find you are asking mostly one type of question or another, vary the proportion and see what happens. If, say, out of thirty questions you ask, three require exploratory talk, decrease the number to one. If you ask thirty questions that require final draft talk, intersperse a few questions that require exploratory talk among them.

Each type of talk has its place. Advocating one to the exclusion of the other would be representative of the usual conversations rather than the contrasting conversations these activities are designed to elicit. Such advocacy would also be learning ways of teaching rather than ways of looking.

Activity 5

In altering the proportion of questions that lead to final draft or exploratory talk, you will see disadvantages of each type of talk. The disadvantages may highlight some features of both types of talk that each contain.

Write some of the disadvantages of each type of talk in the space below, and write features of each type of talk that you noticed that I did not comment on in this section.

[Margin note: Lots to think about as you have Ss engage in both final draft + exploratory talk.]

Disadvantages of final draft talk

Doesn't ask STs to think 'beyond', apply to their own lives. Teacher-centered — it's as if T holds all the 'right' answers. Can lead to monotony and lack of ST interest and participation

Features of final draft talk that you or your partner noticed that I did not comment on

Shows that STs have ability to identify specific details/points of information. Can be used to define vocabulary

Disadvantages of exploratory talk

Can be time-consuming. If the goal is explanation or definition, other STs may become further confused. May possibly jeopardize ST confidence, threaten learner's space. Leads to premature closure of lesson/task

Features of exploratory talk that you or your partner noticed that I did not comment on

reinterpretation — based on one's own meaning making process; threatening — STs may be concerned about being 'wrong' or laughed at (for opinions) by peers

Activity 6

On the lines below, write some other labels, or terms, for final draft talk and exploratory talk. Write terms you consider positive, negative, and neutral, realizing that we each attach our own feelings to words we and others use. Write the labels without your partner so that later you can compare what you each wrote. Writing labels that reflect our feelings can provide an opportunity for each of us to see the feelings attached to the words we use and can provide us with additional features of talk that Barnes' labels alone do not capture.

Terms for final draft talk:

a term with a negative connotation: _closed_

96 ■ Applications of Observing

a term with a positive connotation: _time efficient_
a term with a neutral connotation: _answer provided_
Terms for exploratory talk:
a term with a negative connotation: _disinterested_
a term with a positive connotation: _open-ended_
a term with a neutral connotation: _degree of meaning-making conveyed; usdifference_

Thinking about the Alternatives

If you have a partner you can meet with, compare the terms you each wrote. If you are working alone, leave this work for a few weeks. When you return to it, write some additional terms and compare your initial and subsequent terms. What at one time is netural may at another time seem negative or positive. What to one of us is positive can sometimes be negative-sounding to another.

COMMUNICATION AS A CONTINUUM

Discussion of terms, like indicating whether a communication is exploratory or final draft, often contains comments such as the "on one hand, it is exploratory, but on the other hand, it isn't." Some examples always seem to have some qualities of each characteristic we are dealing with. Even with such a seemingly simple question such as "What color is the Atlantic Ocean on the globe?," we can get a range of responses. The response "Hum—seems to be like the water in the aquarium" shows some features of exploratory talk. The responses "like the water there" and "blue, of course" show fewer. But both show more than "blue" alone.

By placing x for exploratory at one end of a line and f for final draft at the other, and by assigning numbers in between, we can place the communications along a continuum. By using a continuum, we can sometimes capture some of the differences between communications that black-and-white, cut-and-dried binary groupings do not.

A continuum can be thought of as representing exploratory talk and the binary groupings so common in all the sections in this book can be thought of as representing final draft talk. However, fitting communications into either binary groups or along a continuum both produce a great deal of exploratory talk. The continuum shown below can of course be used with any of the groupings in any part of the book by substituting other words that show other features for exploratory and final draft.

```
Exploratory                                              Final draft
   talk                                                      talk
x   1     2     3     4     5     6     7     8     9     10  f
```

You could place a number from 1 to 10 next to a communicaton, depending on whether you think it contains almost all the features of exploratory talk—a 1—or just a few—a 3—or all the features of final draft talk—a 10. For those communications not seeming to fit either, give them a 5.

RECONSIDERING COMPREHENSION

PACKAGING OUR THOUGHTS

Write down the first words that come to your mind after you read the five words listed below. Do not think before you write, just put down the *first* word that comes to your mind after you read each of the following:

bread_____
travel_____
light_____
comprehension_____
reading_____

Here are some words other teachers put next to *comprehension:* understanding, tests, exercises, reading, difficult, listening, questions. The fact that there are a lot of different words that come readily to mind is of course no surprise. Nor are the words that actually spring to mind. If a lot of people consistently had written *blue jay, orange peel,* or *dust cloth,* we might all be surprised. The advantage of these words is that there are single items in the world which we can attach to them. But words like *comprehension, empowerment,* or *whole language* represent many items and concepts. When we use such terms, there is no assurance that our meanings and those of the persons we are talking to are alike.

There is no particular problem with the word *comprehension* per se, or even with any of the associations people make with it. Rather, the problem is with the assumptions we all make that the tasks we consider comprehension tasks are the same tasks others consider comprehension tasks.

Arnheim, who was keenly interested in perception, described the issue in this way:

> Philosophers and scientists constantly struggle with the verbal skills which they must use to package their thoughts.... Should they keep a familiar term and try to invest it with new meanings...? Should they coin a new term? All this trouble arrives because words, as mere labels, try to keep up with the live action of thought taking place in another medium.... The struggle against the words is only a reflection of the true drama going on in thought. To see things in a new light is a genuine cognitive challenge; to adjust the language to the new insight is nothing more than a bothersome technicality.
>
> (Arnheim, 1969, p. 246)

To engage in the "true drama going on in thought," read the passage below. Then, I will give you directions for grouping some tasks that follow the reading. The activity will help us begin to explore the purposes we set for reading tasks.

Three Men, Bread, and Dreams

Once upon a time, three men made an agreement to make a journey together to a distant land. They hoped they could find a life in the distant land which they had not been able to find where they were. They knew the trip was going to be difficult. And, mainly because of this fact, they agreed before they started that they would share everything they had equally during the journey.

After many days of sharing, they were close to their destination. But suddenly they realized that they had not brought enough food and drink along. They had only two loaves of bread and a small flask of wine left. They realized that the remaining food and drink could satisfy only one of them for the last leg of the journey. The other two would have to remain where they were and wait until the one who continued alone would return with food and drink for the two who remained.

They were able to agree that their salvation was only possible if one continued and two remained. If they all tried to travel with such little nourishment, they would likely all perish. But they began to argue about who should continue the journey.

At last, one of the three said, "Let's rest. Perhaps we will fall asleep and dream. In the dream perhaps we will be told who should have the bread and wine and continue the journey." The second traveler agreed. The third said nothing, which the other two interpreted as agreement.

After some time, the traveler who had suggested that they sleep shouted, "I had a dream. In the dream a spirit appeared and said, 'You are the best of the three. You deserve the bread and wine. You should continue the journey for you are the best.'"

"Strange," said the second traveler, who had agreed with the proposal to rest. "In my dream, a spirit came to me. The spirit said, 'You are most likely to complete the journey so take the bread and wine and start immediately.'"

The third traveler burped. He then said, "I was not tired, but I was very hungry and thirsty. So, I ate the bread and drank the wine. Since I now have the most sustenance within me, I will continue the journey." And with that, he got up and started walking towards the city they all hoped to reach.

(Adapted from a tale in *Tales from the Dervishes* by Idries Shah, 1970)

Activity 1

Read the twenty-one tasks below. (There is no need to perform them.) We will work with these tasks in three different ways in this activity.

1. How many men were there?
2. What color is wine usually?
3. What are some words in this reading passage that show it is a story?
4. Underline all the words you don't understand.
5. What is a flask?

Reconsidering Comprehension ■ 99

6. Complete this sentence:

    The third traveler _____

7. Cross out the word that does not belong: I was not tired hungry but I was very hungry and thirsty.

8. Put these words in the right order: wine, bread, of, small, had, they, flask, a, only, and, two, left, loaves, of

9. What type of man was the one who drank the wine and ate the bread?

10. Write another sentence following this pattern: The third traveler burped.

11. Draw a loaf of bread.

12. What did the men agree to share?

13. Do you like wine?

14. Define *share*.

15. Which character do you like best?

16. Cross out any words you don't understand.

17. Translate the first sentence into your first language.

18. Give the main idea of the story.

19. How did you like the story?

20. Retell the story, briefly.

21. Use *burp* in a sentence.

As a first step, separate the twenty-one tasks above into two groups: *comprehension* and *other*. If you want to sort them tactilely as you sorted the stamps by actually moving them about, copy each of the tasks, with its number, on a separate card. Put all the cards you think contain comprehension tasks in one pile and all the others in another pile. Copy the numbers from the cards on the comprehension pile in the first column in the grouping below and the numbers from the other cards in the second column. If you want to sort visually, simply write down the numbers of the tasks you think fit each column.

comprehension	other

Second, have your colleague write down the numbers of the tasks he or she considered comprehension in the left column and those considered other in the second column, just as you did, but using a different colored pen or pencil.

After these two steps, make up any two new pairs of categories based on different characteristics of the items, and divide up all the cards. For example, you may want to note that some questions, as in 1 ("How many men were there?"), begin with question words. Additionally, 1 and some others ask about meaning. Write the titles for your first groupings at the top of the columns in the first T below, next to "Pair 1" and the titles of your second groupings in the second T, next to "Pair 2." Write the numbers of the tasks, as well as the tasks, below the appropriate columns.

As you write your titles or labels on the top of the columns below, perhaps you will begin to see a range of meanings of the word *comprehension* that you did not see before.

Pair 1 _____|_____

Pair 2 _____|_____

Below you will find some groupings that other teachers have made. As a final step, on a separate sheet, copy a few pairs that seem interesting and write the numbers of the tasks that you think fit each.

The purpose of matching your examples with the labels others have given is to see features of the tasks you had not seen before rather than to see whether your perception of the terms and another's is the same.

A.	*involving right hemisphere*	*involving left hemisphere*
B.	*story-related questions*	*non–story-related questions*
C.	*referring to objects or things*	*not referring to objects or things*
D.	*open-ended*	*not open-ended*

Reconsidering Comprehension ■ 101

E.	exploratory	one right answer only
F.	alcohol	no alcohol
G.	important task	unimportant task
H.	personal feelings	no personal feelings
I.	can lead to further interaction	likely to stop interaction
J.	asking for knowledge	asking for comprehension
K.	emphasizing memory	emphasizing more than memory
L.	easy to answer	difficult to answer
M.	likely to lead to a short answer	likely to lead to a long answer
N.	conventional	unconventional
O.	requires one sense	requires more than one sense
P.	oral	not oral

Thinking about the Alternatives

By looking at a range of groupings, you see more clearly the fact that each task has multiple features. Perhaps the groupings you have made will increase your confidence in your perceptions as well.

Groupings do not always neatly accommodate all of the tasks. For example, task 9, "What type of man was the one who drank the wine and ate the bread?," is clearly story-related. But since it also clearly requires some knowledge beyond the story, it is hard to get 100 percent agreement to put task 9 under *story-related questions* in B, alone. This task has features of both of the groupings in B.

Task 19, "How did you like the story?," fits under grouping L, *easy to answer/difficult to answer*. But which side of the grouping is not as clear cut. Easy for the student? Easy from the teacher's point of view? If the teacher is really keen on the student's view, then task 19 also fits under grouping H—*personal feelings/no personal feelings*. But if the teacher is setting the task only to practice a pattern such as "I liked it a lot," then the task has to be put under *no personal feelings*. In short, although we can group each of the twenty-one tasks into many groupings, without the responses of the students and the subsequent reactions of the teachers to the responses, we cannot be sure which characteristic each task has.

By noting a great number of characteristics of the questions we ask when we set reading tasks, the range of areas of knowledge and experience that are required for us to respond to each question becomes evident. If a student failed to comprehend, we might realize that the reason could be a lack of knowledge of the topic, not some general deficiency often diagnosed as a comprehension problem. Knowing this, we could embellish the text during oral reading with explanatory and background comments.

Or a reader might have been so involved comparing personal experiences with one part of the reading that he or she completely forgot another part, thus missing one memory question but not necessarily failing to understand or comprehend and experience perhaps enjoy the reading.

Said another way, if we base our teaching on our diagnosis of students' needs, it is no doubt safer to make a range of specific diagnoses rather than one general one, since in this way we are more likely to set a range of tasks rather than just one type.

*T*HE LIMITS OF THE USUAL CONVERSATIONS

The point of indicating the tenuous nature of the grouping decisions is to remind us all once again of a key limitation of the usual conversations about teaching: the use of single, one-dimensional terms such as *comprehension, easy, important,* and *exploratory*. The single use of such terms leads us to make black-and-white descriptions that fail to reflect the complexity of teaching practices.

Over time, we often begin to group tasks with a particular term whether or not they have the features we originally associated with that term. Each single term becomes a ready-made label rather than an actual descriptor of features of the phenomenon being explored. One of Bateson's conversations with his daughter illustrates how using the same single, one-dimensional term over and over, without frequent reference to the items the term is supposed to describe, and without attention to other features of the same items, often stops us from *seeing*.

> Father: Wait a minute. This is difficult to say.... I think that we get some ideas straight and I think that the muddles help. I mean—that if we both spoke logically all the time, we would only parrot all the old cliches that everybody has repeated for hundreds of years....
>
> Daughter: Yes, Daddy—but what about those things—the ready-made sticks of letters.
>
> Father: The cliches? Yes ... if the printer wants to print something new ... he will have to break up all that old sorting of letters.... In the same way, we have to break up all our ready-made ideas and shuffle the pieces.
>
> (Bateson, 1972, pp. 15, 16)

Regrouping the twenty-one tasks using a range of descriptors, multiple one-dimensional terms rather than single ones, no doubt produced some muddles! Muddles are a central feature of contrasting conversations, just as cliches are a central feature of the usual conversations. Notice that muddles and cliches are not to be equated with the usual or contrasting conversations. The words *usual* and *contrasting* are no different from *comprehension* or any other words we use. They can be taken as one-dimensional and begin to act just like cliches. One aim of the multiple activities in this book is to remind us of the multiple types of things we say in both the usual and contrasting conversations.

Another limitation of the use of single one-dimensional terms such as *comprehension* or *right hemisphere* or *story-related* is that we begin to attach value to each term. If *right hemisphere* has a positive connotation for us, we begin to search for items that fit the term, ignoring other items that do not fit, and ignoring other features of the items that fit.

Terms we attach positive value to often serve as solutions to problems in our discussions. "Oh, if the students can't read well, we need to provide more right hemisphere tasks, or more open-ended tasks, or more tasks that can lead to further interaction." The more value we attach to each single term, and the concepts each tries to represent, the less able we are to see alternatives and the fact that all tasks, like all phenomena, are multi-dimensional.

Here is one person's description of how the process of assigning value to our terms and then using the terms to provide solutions to our problems can stop us from looking:

> Once we have arrived at a solution—and in the process of getting there, have paid a fairly high price in terms of anxiety and expectation—our investment in this solution becomes so great that we may prefer to distort reality to fit our solution rather than sacrifice the solution.
>
> (Watzlawick, 1977, p. 54)

Activity 2

Determining characteristics of tasks in isolation is useful for generating characteristics. But for matching characteristics to the tasks, we need to see them being performed.

To that end, visit your colleague's class or listen to a tape from his or her class or your own. Write down a half dozen tasks that the students were asked to do along with their responses. Then, match the characteristics that intrigue you from the earlier groupings, or new characteristics the new tasks suggest. After seeing the tasks the students were asked to perform as well as their responses, you could try altering the proportion of tasks. For example, if you found a number of the tasks that emphasized memory were difficult to answer and were oral, you might want to see whether having students write memory questions affected their difficulty. Having students write responses to questions that tended to lead to short answers would allow you to see the effect of writing on this feature of questions as well.

ONE PERSON'S DEFINITION OF COMPREHENSION

Obviously the sixteen groupings above—A through P pairs of characteristics—are too many to deal with at one time. But they remind us of the multiple characteristics of all communications. And they point out that any one-dimensional grouping of tasks fails to reveal the richness, the complexity, and the ambiguity of the tasks we set.

But does noting multiple characteristics of reading and listening tasks tell us what comprehension really is? Well, what comprehension really is and whether we can see it happening are two different things. Frank Smith, among others, defines comprehension in a way that I, John, "comprehend." But I am not sure what tasks you can give me to show you that I, in fact, comprehend what I say I comprehend.

At any rate, here is what Frank Smith has to say. He defines comprehension as "making sense." (Smith, 1975, p. 10) He goes on to say

> Comprehension is the condition of having cognitive questions answered, the absence of uncertainty.... Comprehension exists, in other words, when there is no residual uncertainty.... It is true that we comprehend any situation, verbal or otherwise, by relating it to what we already know ... but how often do we want to become aware of everything we know about a word or object that we see? If the topic of concern happens to be colors, then I want to recall that milk is white. If the concern is with the cost of living, then I want to remember the price of milk and the rate at which my family consumes it. Certainly if I am drinking milk for refreshment, the last thing I want to think of is the udder of a cow. In brief, we do not comprehend indiscriminately, but rather in terms of what we are looking for.... The true art of making sense of the world lies in knowing what can be safely ignored.
>
> (Smith, 1975, pp. 34, 35)

Activity 3

Given Smith's comments, another way to look at the twenty-one tasks is to see which of them leads readers to know "what can be safely ignored."

Go back to the twenty-one tasks in Activity 1 on pages 99–100 and write *s i* for *safely ignore* next to those items that you think lead readers to learn to ignore what is not central, what can be safely ignored.

Then write *f a* for *focus attention* next to those items that you think lead readers to treat all items in a reading passage with equal attention and suggest that we can ignore items only at our peril.

If possible, invite a partner to compare the places you both put *s i* and *f a*. As you compare feelings about which items taught people to ignore what was not important, discuss the process you used to come to your decision. Did you rethink your "safely ignore" labels as you wrote "focus attention" and change some of your original labels? Said another way, what did *you* focus attention on and what did you safely ignore in labeling the tasks?

Thinking about the Alternatives

If we were to rewrite the items you marked with *f a*—those items which fail to aid readers in determining what to ignore because they focus attention on everything and give equal weight to everything—we could quite easily generate a wide range of alternative tasks. For example, item 4, which seems to focus attention on all the words—"Underline all the words you don't understand"—could be rewritten like so: "After you underline all the words you don't understand, cross out those you think you can ignore and you don't have to look up in a dictionary."

And item 5—"What is a flask?"—which suggests that *flask* cannot be safely ignored—could be asked in this way: "After telling me what a flask is, tell me whether you need to know what a flask is to understand the story."

Activity 4

Now go to the groupings of the tasks in Activity 1 (pages 101–102). First, mark with a plus sign those groupings you made as well as the groupings others have made in which at least one of the pairs has what you think is a positive connotation. For example, *personal feelings* to me is positive, as is *open-ended*. Then, compare your ratings with your partner. Of course, some will be neither positive nor negative.

Read the pairs again that you both agreed were positive types of tasks and see which pairs of characteristics are important, given Frank Smith's comments, and which are not. Cross out groupings others have made as well as your own that you think characterize tasks that are detrimental to comprehension, given Frank Smith's comments.

I hasten to remind you that you are not being asked to determine what tasks are detrimental to comprehension. You are simply being asked to compare beliefs and practices: Frank Smith's belief as quoted in this section and some practices illustrated by the twenty-one tasks.

RELATING THE CLASSROOM TO THE OUTSIDE WORLD

BRINGING OUTSIDE BEHAVIORS INTO THE CLASSROOM

One of the most frequent teacher questions I have observed *inside* classrooms around the world is "What's this?" The question is asked as the teacher holds up an object. Related questions—"What's that?" "What're these?" "What're those?" "What color is it?" "What's it made of?" "What do you call this?"—are also common. These questions are also frequently asked *outside* of classrooms, among the students. But the characteristics of the questions we ask inside the classroom as teachers and outside the classroom as learners are often different. For example:

INSIDE THE CLASSROOM:	The person asking the questions knows the answer, if the person is a teacher.
OUTSIDE THE CLASSROOM:	The person asking the question usually does not know the answer—is seeking information.
OR, INSIDE THE CLASSROOM:	Often ten or more different objects are asked about in a few minutes.
OUTSIDE THE CLASSROOM:	Usually only one or two items are asked about at a time (within a few minutes).

To provide students with opportunities to ask and answer questions in the classroom that can prepare them to meet needs they will have outside of the classroom, we can substitute "outside" questions for "inside" questions. But before we do, we need to know how each differs from the other.

Throughout this section you will find some drawings with numbers and blank lines. Later on, we'll come back to these to discover what they point out about "askers" and "answerers."

1. _____

Activity 1

Observe the use of the "What's this?" mode of questioning inside and outside classrooms. You may in fact find some examples on the recordings you made of your stamp grouping in Part One. Then, in the spaces below, write down some characteristics of the question or the questioning scene that you observe in both situations, even if they are similar to those noted above. If you are able to catch what both people say or do after the

Relating the Classroom to the Outside World ■ 107

questions have been asked and answered, note these communications in the bottom of the spaces, under *after the questions*.

inside	outside

after the questions

STEPS FOR INCORPORATING OUTSIDE CHARACTERISTICS INSIDE A CLASS

Noting characteristics of communications is an important first step to understanding teaching practices. But knowing characteristics alone does not usually lead to changes in practices. In order to generate changes in our practices from our observations, a number of steps are necessary.

First, we have to realize that adding out-of-class characteristics of questions to in-class questions requires contrivance. There is no way to duplicate out-of-class activites in the classroom naturally. Teaching is a contrivance.

With this realization in mind, the second step simply requires that we note features of an out-of-class characteristic—a distinctive feature—one at a time. Then, we have to note a comparable feature with the same characteristic as our in-class communications. Noting the most obvious features of a characteristic of out-of-class communications and how our in-class communications are different is often the easiest way to begin. Passing over the obvious features of characteristics for less obvious ones, which might seem more sophisticated, can make the comparisons and subsequent substitutions more complex than they need to be. Often, the first features of each characteristic we note and then substitute will be ones that require that we do the exact opposite of what we normally do. The obvious fact that we tend to know the answer to questions we ask in class and not know the answer outside of class exemplifies this idea of opposites.

Modifying Three Characteristics

To illustrate these steps, below are noted three characteristics of questions often seen when we ask about objects outside a classroom. Beneath each characteristic are listed the steps for making it possible to incorporate each characteristic into questions we ask inside a classroom.

Characteristic 1: Position of People Asking and Answering Questions

1. Note the position of people asking and answering questions outside of class: Both Person A and Person B are in the same position, either both standing or both sitting.
2. Note the position of people asking and answering questions inside of class: Person A is standing and Person B is sitting; or, Person A is standing and Person B is sitting when addressed but told to stand to state the response and then sit down again.
3. Note the difference between the positions: Out of class, both are in the same position; in class, both are in different positions at least part of the time.
4. Substitute the out-of-class position for the one in-class position: Before questions are started, ask all students to stand and keep standing as the questions are asked and answered.

Characteristic 2: Number of People Observing the Interaction

1. Note the number of people in the area around those asking and answering the questions outside of the classroom: Person A, asking for the name of an object or other information, often does so in the presence of only one other person. Person A may be talking to a clerk in a store, for example. Even if other customers are close by in this setting, they usually number only three or four.
2. Note the number of people in the area around those asking and answering the questions inside of class: The entire class usually makes up the audience for questions asked and answered in classrooms; if there are 10 students in the class, 9 are observing the person answering the question; if there are 50 students, 49 are.
3. Note the difference between the numbers in both settings: There are few observed or involved out of class and many in class.
4. Substitute the out-of-class numbers for the in-class numbers: Have students ask questions of each other in pairs, so that each student who asks a question has only one other person listening and likewise with the person answering—in each case, only the partner with whom the student is interacting.

Characteristic 3: Purpose of Person in Asking the Question

1. Note the purpose of the person asking questions outside of class: to seek some information the person does not know.
2. Note the purpose of the person asking questions inside the class: to see if the person answering knows the information; the person asking the question already knows the information but is checking to see whether the other person knows the same information.
3. Note the difference between the purposes inside and outside of the classroom: outside, the purpose is to seek information, while inside, the purpose is to check students' retention, understanding, attention, or involvement.

4. Substitute the out-of-class characteristic for the in-class characteristic: (a) teacher writes the names of a number of objects on one set of note cards; (b) teacher draws sketches of the objects on a separate set of note cards; (c) teacher passes out note cards with names of objects to some students and other characteristics of objects to other students; (d) teacher passes out note cards with sketches of objects to other students; (e) teacher tells students holding cards with sketches to find a student holding a card with names or other information about sketches and then to ask for information about the sketches.

The steps would be no different if we were interested in redesigning stamps. We could list features of all those stamps we liked and all those we did not like. Then, after noting some differences and similarities, we could substitute features from stamps we liked for features on stamps we did not like. Since stamps contain pictures of people and things from the world, we could also look for features in other pictorial materials we liked and substitute some of these for those on stamps we decided we did not like.

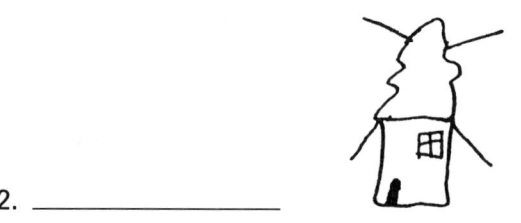

2. _____

Activity 2

One of the characteristics noted in *after the questions*, in Activity 1 above, is the type of comment that is made by the person who asks the questions. Using this characteristic, write down the steps to follow in order to incorporate out-of-class reactions in class.

> Characteristic: Type of comments made by person who asks the question after the question is answered
> _____
> _____
> _____
> _____
> _____
> _____
> _____
> _____

Considering Steps Developed by Others

Steps another pair of teachers developed are printed below so you can compare your steps with those of others.

1. Note out-of-class feature of reaction: Person who asked the question makes comments such as these after the question has been answered: "Oh, I hadn't heard that before;" "Now, I remember," or, "Strange sound." Often, a tone of excitement or pleasure is heard in the comments.

2. Note in-class feature of reaction: Person who asked the question makes comments such as these after the question has been answered: "O.K.," "Glad to see you're paying attention," or, "Very good." The comments are often said in a neutral tone of voice.

3. Note difference between in-class and out-of-class feature of reaction: There is more variation in the words used in out-of-class reactions and there is a greater range of emotions communicated.

4. Substitute an out-of-class feature for an in-class feature:

    a. On note cards, teacher writes comments heard outside of class made by those who ask questions after the questions have been answered;

    b. Teacher holds cards in hands when asking questions in class;

    c. When a student names an object or gives other information the teacher is checking, the teacher reads a reaction from one of the note cards in a neutral tone of voice;

    d. After reading a reaction, teacher shuffles the cards to make it less likely that the same reaction will be read a second time immediately after it has been read the first time;

    e. After a student names an object or gives other information the teacher is checking, the teacher reads the words on one of the cards silently; the teacher then looks at the student and says the words with a tone of voice expressing interest, excitement, lethargy, or some other emotion.

3. _____

Activity 3

As you incorporate some out-of-class characteristics into your teaching, you no doubt anticipate some reactions from both your students and yourself. For example, reading comments from note cards after students answer your questions may make you feel uncomfortable at first. Or, having all students stand up and talk to each other in pairs with what are essentially cue cards may make you wonder whether you are necessary in the class. Write below some reactions you anticipate if you incorporate some similar changes.

_____
_____
_____
_____
_____
_____
_____

Thinking about Possible Reactions

Below is what a couple of teachers wrote about reactions they expected to hear after incorporating almost any of the outside characteristics of questions inside their classes. Compare the reactions you listed with these two. And if your partner wrote some, compare yours with your partner's as well.

> Students will be confused—they won't know if they are right or wrong if I don't say "O.K." or "Very good." They won't pay attention if I don't remind some that it is important with a comment such as "Glad to see you're paying attention."
>
> Students won't understand my comments and will think that showing excitement after they respond is artificial.

4. _____

Activity 4

Actually try out one of the characteristics noted in either Activity 1 or 2 that you would like to incorporate in your teaching. Then, after the lesson, write below your reactions and the reactions to the substitution of the features of that characteristic. Student reactions can be simply your interpretations of how they reacted. Or, you could ask the students to write comments on any changes they observed, noting what they liked about the changes and what they did not like.

Finally, compare the actual reactions with your expected reactions and record them in the space provided. Then take a moment to think about the effects of the features of characteristics of questions you substituted in comparison with the effects of the usual features. In your reflections, you might want to comment also on the value of generating alternative teaching practices by comparing out-of-class and in-class communications using the steps you just read and tried to follow.

Expected reactions to an *outside* characteristic *inside* a class

_____
_____
_____
_____
_____

Actual reactions to alternative way of asking questions

_____
_____
_____
_____

Differences between expected and actual reactions to alternative way of asking questions

_____
_____
_____
_____
_____

Similarities between expected and actual reactions to alternative way of asking questions

_____
_____
_____
_____
_____

Value of generating alternative teaching practices by comparing out-of-class and in-class communications

_____
_____
_____
_____
_____

Thinking about Reactions

Here is what some other teachers wrote:

> I enjoy questions more when I ask them in class with the tone of voice and facial expressions that reflect the curiosity, embarrassment, or other emotions that I observe people show when they ask questions outside of class.

> Making side comments in place of "O.K., very good" provides my students with a lot of vocabulary. They often wonder what the words mean exactly. But they sense I have heard them give their answers and am reacting personally to them rather than automatically. When they ask about words they do not understand, they are asking questions the way we do outside the classroom—they don't know the answer!

> I ask fewer questions about objects than I used to. I have students ask each other now. This allows me to listen to more students, and frees me from trying to be curious when I ask students to remember colors or qualities of objects. I always felt insincere and phoney when I asked students to give me answers I already knew.

SWITCHING PLACES: CHARACTERISTICS OF NAMING TASKS FROM THE LEARNER'S POINT OF VIEW

Let's take on the perspective and filters of a student. Now note characteristics of "What's this?" from the point of view of the person answering the question. But first, you need to see the question and respond to it.

5. _____

Activity 5

Go back now to the sketches placed throughout this section and on the blank line next to each write down what you want to call the sketch. After you have done this for each, write below some characteristics of the task of titling the sketches, from the point of view of a learner.

_____
_____
_____
_____

Thinking about the Alternatives

Seeing the types of things other people wrote shows how they interpreted the direction "write down what you want to call the sketch." Here are some alternatives—and perhaps some contrasting observations.

1. a hut; a design in black and white

2. a house with TV aerials; makes me want a cold drink with foam on top

3. a mushroom with insects on it; crazy sketch

4. a tomb; reminds me of a Greek island with those whitewashed houses

5. a silo; Mickey Mouse ears turn up all over the place these days

As you can see, some people tended to think they were expected to name the objects, and so wrote down inside classroom characteristics. They seemed to take the words "what you want to call the sketch" literally, and so wrote down names for the objects they thought the sketches might represent.

Others seemed to think they could write down what came to their minds. Thus, after the nouns that name the pictures, there are words representing other things that came to them. Some people wrote both types of comments after each sketch.

The words in the directions of course are ambiguous, as most words are. Much of our schooling is spent trying to figure out from the words a teacher says what answer we are supposed to give. We need to figure out what the teacher expects—what is likely—given past expectations.

MATCHING INTENTIONS AND PERCEPTIONS OF INTENTIONS

Given the usual intentions of asking about objects inside classrooms, it is thus not surprising for learners to fit the words to perceived intentions. Mismatching between the teacher's intentions and the learner's understanding of the intentions as the teacher expresses them in words is not really different from one of the points Cervantes makes in the classic windmill scene in *Don Quixote*. In that scene, reprinted below, Sancho seems to think that the way to see the world is as it is. Don Quixote sees the world through his knighthood visor. In a way, Sancho's claim that windmills are windmills and not giants represents questions and answers as we normally deal with them in the classroom—with right answers. Don Quixote's claim that the windmills are giants is closer to many of the questions and answers as we normally deal with them outside of the classroom: more options are possible, multiple interpretations are possible.

> At that moment they caught sight of some thirty or forty windmills, which stand on that plain, and as soon as Don Quixote saw them he said to his squire: "Fortune is guiding our affairs better than we could have wished. Look over there, friend Sancho Panza, where more than thirty monstrous giants appear. I intend to do battle with them and take all their lives. . . ."
>
> "What giants?" asked Sancho Panza.
>
> "Those you see there," replied his master, "with their long arms. Some giants have them about six miles long."
>
> "Take care, your worship," said Sancho; "those things over there are not giants but windmills, and what seem to be their arms are the sails, which are whirled round in the wind and make the millstone turn."
>
> "It is quite clear," replied Don Quixote, "that you are not experienced in this matter of adventures. They are giants, and if you are afraid, go away and say your prayers, whilst I advance and engage them in fierce and unequal battle."
>
> (pt. 1, chap. 8)

What answer did I want you to write on the lines? What was my intention in asking you to write words on the lines below the sketches? My intention, as I said, was at least in part to illustrate the ambiguity that is possible in almost any communication. The instruction I gave to the child who drew the sketches was simply: "Draw some windmills." Whether you thought from the beginning that the sketches represented windmills or not, since the windmill quote came after you were asked to write words on the blanks, there is no reason to consider yourself silly if you wrote "monsters" or some other words that might be less literal. On the other hand, realizing that the sketches were windmills before reading the quote I hope does not make you feel particularly clever. Nor would I want you to feel original if you wrote "trademark," "movement," or other words that came to your mind. Given the ambiguity of the direction, any words are not only acceptable but welcome.

If you are used to feeling frustrated when students do not answer the question you think you asked—whether in class or on a test—see if the experience of writing words below the sketches reminds you of the fact that the unexpected answer can show as much thinking, maybe more than the expected answer. And when an unexpected answer comes, it is not necessarily because of our words alone but because of other characteristics of words, such as interest or enthusiasm, or lethargy—as well as our intentions and those of the person responding.

Conversely, if you are used to accepting any words said, no matter what the question, see if the experience of writing words below the sketches in this section reminds you that being free to use many words to name an object, rather than simply coming up with the name of the object the person asking the question has in mind, can be just as gratifying as stating the word the person has in mind. When talking about an object or sketch does the chance to play with words—monster, trademark, hut—provide some of the same feelings that coming up with the expected word—windmill—does? Just as Sancho Panza and Don Quixote would both have had larger visions of reality if each could have seen what the other saw, so each of us can profit from the views of those we interact with, inside and outside of the classroom.

QUESTIONS AS ONE EXAMPLE OF WHAT A TEACHER DOES

Over time, following the steps given in Activity 2 provides a way to incorporate in-class features of outside-of-class questions. One feature every few weeks is less likely to be upsetting than trying many features all at once. And, as you try alternatives, continue to write down your reactions and those of your students.

As you have no doubt guessed by now, questions are a metaphor for any classroom activity we do. Comparing characteristics of the ways we read and listen to language in classrooms and other teaching settings, such as libraries, with the ways we read and listen to language outside of teaching settings, such as on trains, in our living rooms, and at concerts or movies, can provide other ideas of alternative practices in our classrooms.

Tape-recording a group of chemists working in a lab and juxtaposing the way they talk about an experiment with the way we talk about experiments in our classrooms will reveal a range of options we can try in our classrooms. Listening to some bankers discuss profit and loss, interest rates, and budgets can suggest a range of ways we can discuss mathematics differently in our math class.

Comparing classroom conversations and activities in the various disciplines and subjects with out-of-class conversations on these topics will remind us of how school knowledge and world knowledge overlap as well as remain distinct in a number of ways. (Barnes, 1976, p. 79)

Are you puzzled or confused as you explore out-of-class communications? Are you and your students confused by directives such as "write what you want to call the sketch"? If so, consider whether the usual negative reaction to confusion is not perhaps a bit one-sided. Weigh the possible value of such feelings. Look at the extent to which the claim about the value of confusion in the quotation below is valid.

> It might seem that there is nothing good about confusion, but this is not quite the case. Suppose everybody starts laughing as I enter a room. This is very confusing to me because the others either see the reality of the situation very differently than I do or are in possession of some information that I do not have. My immediate reaction is to search for

clues—from looking to see if somebody is behind me to wondering if they have just been talking about me; from going to a mirror to see if I have a smudge on my face to demanding an explanation.

After the initial shock, confusion triggers off an immediate search for meaning or order to reduce the anxiety inherent in any uncertain situation. The result is an unusual increase in attention. . . . In other words, confusion sharpens our sense and our attention to detail.

(Watzlawick, 1977, p. 27)

Remember what we said in the Introduction to this book: Uncertainty can lead us to new understanding.

SELECTING AND USING MATERIALS

Many of us remember the story of Newton's insights into the force of gravity from the story about his observation of a falling apple. But Bronowski reminds us that Newton's insight into gravity was not that he saw an apple falling from a tree; millions of people had seen apples fall from trees before Newton and supposed some force caused the apples to fall. Bronowski tells us that Newton's insight was seeing an apple fall on a moonlit night and realizing that the round moon and the round apple were pulled by the same force. The apple fell to the ground and the moon kept in orbit around the earth because they were each pulled by the force of gravity.

We could say that his insight came from grouping two seemingly different phenomena in the same category. To Bronowski, the central, if not only, aim of science and art is to see such "hidden likenesses." We see what we did not see before, discovering "a new order which gives unity to what had long seemed unlike" partly by comparing items that seem different, two seemingly contrasting elements. (Bronowski, 1956, p. 15)

REFRESHING OUR VISION

I think most would agree that at least at first glance the patch of cloth shown on the cover and the stamps included in this book are "two seemingly contrasting elements." The cloth is made of cotton; the stamps of paper. The cloth is placed on furniture or people in the form of clothes, the stamps on envelopes.

While it is obvious that trying to put a piece of cloth on an envelope to substitute for a postage stamp and stamps on a hole in a shirt to substitute for a patch of cloth is unlikely to be productive, seeing similarities between seemingly different items may do more than enable us to see "a new order which gives unity to what had long seemed unlike." Grouping the same items in a range of ways might provide us with an opportunity to see features, in this case of materials, that we might have missed before because, among other reasons, the features were so obvious.

Bateson offers this explanation for the difficulty of seeing something obvious:

> [People often miss the obvious] because people are self-corrective systems. They are self-corrective against disturbance, and if the obvious is not of a kind that [we] can easily assimilate without internal disturbance, [our] self-corrective mechanisms work to sidetrack it, to hide it, even to the extent of shutting the eyes if necessary, or shutting off various parts of the process of perception. Disturbing information can be framed like a pearl so that it doesn't make a nuisance of itself. . . .
>
> (Bateson, 1972, p. 428)

Activity 1

To encourage fresh looking at our use of common materials, I've written below the names of the places where certain materials are usually used. As you read the list of items found in each setting, select two or three settings of particular interest to you and circle items in those settings that you would like to add to the classroom you use.

1. Writer's desk:
    scotch tape, a typewriter, scissors, pencils and erasers, note cards with notes on them, a dictionary, a word processor, books lying on the desk, a desk with a padded chair by it on wheels, a radio, white-out, stamps

2. Nursery school or kindergarten:
    colored crayons, dolls, easels with large white sheets of paper on them, watercolors and brushes, toys, a sand box, an aquarium, rabbit cage and hamster cage, large plants, small mats on the floor and a carpeted area, dried leaves glued on pieces of paper tacked on a large bulletin board which covers half of the side of one wall, photographs of those in the room on the bulletin board along with sketches of the same faces, a piano, a small counter with cups on it and crackers, a wash basin and sink next to the counter, pieces of cloth

3. English or social studies classroom:
    a chalkboard, rows of seats with desks attached, window shades, a clock with hands on its face, a framed picture of a former political leader of the country above the chalkboard in the front of the room, a flag, a desk with a small bell on it in the front of the room with a chair in front of it facing the rows of seats, a loud speaker mounted in the wall next to the picture of the political leader, a phonograph, some maps on the wall, travel posters, textbooks locked in book shelves with glass doors along one wall

4. Living room in an apartment:
    a VCR, a video camera, a phonograph, disc and tape player, radio sound system with speakers, a television set, a couch and three upholstered chairs, carpeted floor, drapes at the edges of the windows, some framed photographs, paintings and illustrations on the walls, floor lamps, a desk with a barometer on it and two books with reproductions of paintings, a tray with stamps in it, some envelopes with stationery and pens next to the tray, three straight-backed chairs (one by the desk), the desk facing the wall, a digital clock on a drum table, six plants in pots of various sizes, the largest pot 1 meter in diameter, the smallest one 20 centimeters, a camera, catalogs from department, clothing, and electronic stores

5. Bookstore or library:
    shelves from floor to ceiling (8 feet), half filled with books, labels on the edges of the shelves, two shelves with folded maps on

them, a bookcase around 3 feet high with a counter on top holding book catalogs, a large table with small piles of books on it, quiet classical music heard from speakers, some illustrations on blank parts of the walls in between the shelves

6. Kitchen:
cans of fruit, fresh oranges, boxes of cookies, a stove, a counter, a sink, dishes, potato chips, a bag of chocolate-chip cookies, three straight chairs, one small table, plates, silverware, a refrigerator, cabinets with soap in them

As some people begin to circle items, the number of items becomes so great that they begin to wonder why they have so few items in their own classrooms. And they begin to wonder why schools can't have a few more classrooms that are like living rooms. Or at least they wonder why some items from living rooms cannot be added to classrooms. Some who teach older students wonder why only nursery schools and kitchens and writers' desks have items that learners of any age could use.

Others circle only a few items and wonder why even the English/social studies classroom has so much equipment. Some argue that maps, globes, and pictures—to say nothing of music—are distracting and make it more difficult for students to concentrate on reading, listening, and writing. They consider the "additional" items frills.

Activity 2

Whether you see classrooms as places that are starved of the range of items we experience outside of classrooms, or as appropriately furnished and equipped, for this activity group items in different settings in a range of ways to perhaps see some hidden likenesses. Either alone or with a partner, take at least ten items from the settings just described and list as many as will fit in the pairs of columns below.

contribute to learning	do not contribute to learning

likely to be stolen	not likely to be stolen

made to entertain	not made to entertain

childish	not childish

difficult to keep in working order	not difficult to keep in working order

expensive	not expensive

Exploring Alternatives

Now, from the pairs of columns in the grouping you just completed insert the negative words and prefixes in the titles of the right-hand columns (i.e., *do not, not*) in front of the appropriate words in the titles of the left-hand columns. Then cross out the negatives in the titles of the right-hand columns. In short, make the meaning of each title of each column the exact opposite of what it was when you started.

Once you have reversed the meaning of each column title, select one item listed in the left-hand column and try to give a reason in the space below why the item could have an attribute exactly the opposite of the attribute you and your partner originally assigned to it. For example, take an item such as upholstered chairs, which most of us initially put under *do not contribute to learning*, and state how upholstered chairs may fit under the title *contribute to learning*. Take an item such as crayons, which usually winds up in the *childish* column and state at least one way crayons can be adult, or suitable for teens in a class. Consider how a VCR or a video camera, which among some American teachers most often is thought of as an item likely to be stolen, and develop a way of using them that may lead to decreased stealing of many items.

_____
_____
_____
_____
_____

Selecting and Using Materials

_____
_____
_____
_____

Thinking about the Alternatives

Here are a few reasons other people put down.

> Students who develop a play that is video recorded and played back in class might become protective of the equipment. Plants and animals that have to be cared for might bring some to school who feel overwhelmed by books and the usual school things. Upholstered chairs in a corner of a classroom might provide a relaxing setting for some; some might be reminded of the fact that reading is not only for a nursery school. The chairs might be enjoyed while reading in class as well as while having a snack. In an advanced science class, crayons can be used to draw cells seen through a microscope so that the borders of the cells and the colors of parts of the cells can be more accurately copied. Many texts have pictures in color but after the first couple of years in school, few students have the chance to reflect in the note-taking and sketching they do in school the range of colors they actually see.

What are Visual Aids?

None of us has heard anyone ever say "look at my new audiovisual aids" when a friend shows us new video equipment, cameras, or sound equipment in an apartment! We consider these items part of the network of communications we take in or use. In a science lab or in an apartment, a barometer is not an "audiovisual aid," but an instrument that measures air pressure in a way that can suggest changes in the weather.

To the extent to which we consider equipment *aids*, we may be limited in our vision of their uses. In an apartment, as in some bookstores, or in the writer's office, equipment that we flick on is not an audio aid. We regard these items as part of the network of communications we are part of. In the same way, pictures on our walls, as those in museums and magazines, are not considered visual aids. Why not consider bringing the outside world into the classroom in terms of materials?

DESIGNING A CLASS SETTING

Activity 3

Below are some additional categories in which to list items from the settings described in Activity 1. By listing some items under a column with labels that are not frequently used we may see some characteristics of materials we did not see before, thus discovering Bronowski's "new order which gives unity to what had long seemed unlike."

Rather than listing some items in one grouping and other items in another grouping, which is the usual task, select around a dozen items from the six settings and put these items in one side of each of the eight separate pairs of columns below. For example, if you select catalogs, put it under one of the columns in one of *each* of the eight pairs of categories: either *hard* or *soft*, *produced to sell products* or *produced to teach something*, and so forth. Don't put catalogs under only one column of a pair and a radio under one side of another pair, and so on.

hard	soft

produced to sell products	produced to teach something

for pleasure	for other purposes

alive	not alive

beautiful to look at or listen to	not beautiful to look at or listen to

can be manipulated	cannot be manipulated

found only in schools	found in many settings

rare/difficult to obtain	common/easy to obtain

Activity 4

Now go back to the items you have just selected and grouped in the eight pairs of columns, and next to items that you think are usually associated with teaching write a *t* for teaching.

On the short lines on the left below, copy two or three items you marked with a *t*. Copy the words above the column the items appear in on the long lines on the right as well.

As an example, here are items other teachers marked with a *t*: textbooks and maps. Textbooks were listed under the column headed *hard* and maps under the category *soft* in the same T. They were both listed under the column *produced to teach something*.

textbooks—*t*:	hard; produced to teach something; for other purposes; not alive; not beautiful to look at; cannot be manipulated; found only in schools; expensive
maps—*t*:	soft; produced to teach something; for other purposes; not alive; not beautiful to look at; can be manipulated; found only in schools; expensive
_____—*t*:	_____
_____—*t*:	_____
_____—*t*:	_____

Activity 5

What about the items that you did not mark with a *t*? Take three of them and copy each one on the broken lines below. Then on the long blank lines write the titles from the columns in the eight T's that apply to the items you copied. The eight titles will indicate eight characteristics of the items. (One example is done here to illustrate the task.)

potato chips:	hard, produced to sell products, for pleasure, not alive, not beautiful to look at, can be manipulated, found in many settings, common—easy to obtain
_____ :	_____
_____ :	_____

124 ■ Applications of Observing

| **Activity 6** | Complete the title "My Ideal Classroom for Teaching..." by filling in a subject you normally teach. Then draw a picture of your own classroom, as it is. With crayons or colored pencils, or some sort of writing utensil you do not usually use, cross out or partially obscure items you would like to remove from your classroom—if there are any such items. And then draw in items you would like to add to your classroom. In short, create your ideal classroom—as far as its materials. |

My Ideal Classroom for Teaching _ _ _ _ _ _ _ _ _ _ _ _ _ _ _ _

With your partner, if possible, list below a few of the items you crossed out, in the appropriate columns (below). Do the same with those items you added.

hard	soft
produced to sell products	produced to teach something
for pleasure	for other purposes
alive	not alive
beautiful to look at or listen to	not beautiful to look at or listen to
can be manipulated	cannot be manipulated
found only in schools	found in many settings
rare/difficult to obtain	common/easy to obtain

Thinking about the Alternatives

Here is John's ideal classroom for teaching languages:

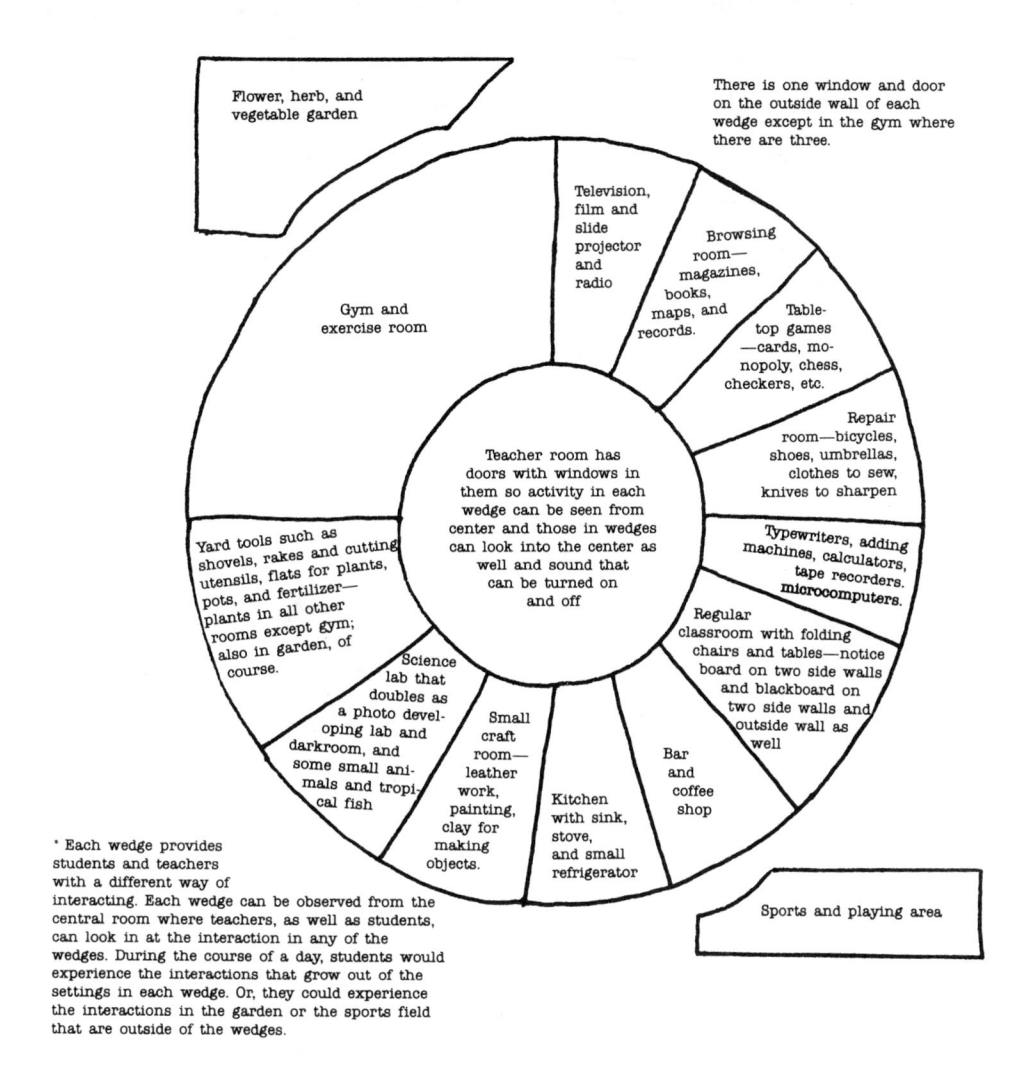

Flower, herb, and vegetable garden

There is one window and door on the outside wall of each wedge except in the gym where there are three.

Gym and exercise room

Television, film and slide projector and radio

Browsing room—magazines, books, maps, and records.

Table-top games—cards, monopoly, chess, checkers, etc.

Teacher room has doors with windows in them so activity in each wedge can be seen from center and those in wedges can look into the center as well and sound that can be turned on and off

Repair room—bicycles, shoes, umbrellas, clothes to sew, knives to sharpen

Yard tools such as shovels, rakes and cutting utensils, flats for plants, pots, and fertilizer—plants in all other rooms except gym; also in garden, of course.

Typewriters, adding machines, calculators, tape recorders, microcomputers.

Regular classroom with folding chairs and tables—notice board on two side walls and blackboard on two side walls and outside wall as well

Science lab that doubles as a photo developing lab and darkroom, and some small animals and tropical fish

Small craft room—leather work, painting, clay for making objects.

Kitchen with sink, stove, and small refrigerator

Bar and coffee shop

Sports and playing area

* Each wedge provides students and teachers with a different way of interacting. Each wedge can be observed from the central room where teachers, as well as students, can look in at the interaction in any of the wedges. During the course of a day, students would experience the interactions that grow out of the settings in each wedge. Or, they could experience the interactions in the garden or the sports field that are outside of the wedges.

*S*UMMING UP THE BEGINNING

If you have a recording of any of the conversations you have had during this section, listen to it for awhile and see if there are any times when either you or another person shows some excitement at discovery. Transcribe the lines below (or, if you have no tape for this section, write down a generalization or an insight about materials that you and your partner grouped).

Share your discovery with others. Almost any material can be used to teach almost anything if we remember that the discipline the material was designed to teach is in fact a part of a large universe of disciplines.

_____
_____
_____
_____
_____
_____
_____
_____
_____

STARTING CLASS

To some, the few minutes we use to start our classes are trivial, in both the actual amount of time spent and the significance of the activities. In this section of the book we are, however, reminded of the interrelationships among various teaching practices: making a change in one area can have a profound effect in another. Though a general might be more important on a battlefield than a nail, the anecdote that ends with "for want of a nail the battle was lost" ("For want of a nail, the shoe was lost, for want of a shoe, the horse was lost, for want of a . . .") reminds us that one small element can profoundly affect the outcomes of many events. A small patch of ice on a highway can cause a half dozen cars to spin out of control and stop traffic for hours. Seemingly small things can have multiple effects out of all proportion to the size or amount of time or apparent importance of the events themselves.

In addition to illustrating the interrelationships among various practices, the steps in the activities in this section, like the steps for grouping stamps, can be applied to any practice you wish to explore.

WAYS OF GREETING STUDENTS

Activity 1

Below are six practices that I have seen teachers use to greet students at the beginning of class. Circle the numbers of any practices you follow, realizing that within each practice there is some variation and that it is unlikely that two different teachers follow the same practices in an identical way.

1. TEACHER: Good morning, class.

    [Said in neutral voice to entire class, standing behind the desk in the front of the classroom]

    CLASS: Good morning teacher.

    [Said like a chant, standing at desks, eyes on desks]

2. TEACHER: How are you?

    [Said in neutral voice to entire class, standing in front of class, eyes on textbook on desk]

    CLASS: Fine thank you.

    [Said in a chant, sitting at desks, eyes looking at various places, but not at teacher]

3. TEACHER: How are you?

    [Said with interest and energy, addressed to one student, standing at blackboard and inviting student to say a word that represents his or her feeling by pointing to the following three sketches]

f _ _ e   s _ _ o   t _ _ _ _ _ _ e

    STUDENT: Terrible!
    [Said with a tone that reflects the meaning of the word]
    TEACHER: And you?
    [Said with interest to another student, pointing to board to indicate the student should choose]
    STUDENT: So so.
    [Said with neutral expression on face]
4. TEACHER: I feel tired today—anyone else feel tired?
    [Said while leaning against the wall, looking at class. Then, the teacher looks at the blackboard to indicate the following expressions that are written there]

No, _ _ _ a bit.   Not really.   I do.   I'm bushed.

    [Then the teacher looks at the class again]
    How about you, Tadashi?
    STUDENT: No, not a bit.
    TEACHER: Atsushi?
    STUDENT: I do. I'm bushed.
5. TEACHER: [Writes these items on the blackboard]
    How are you?

    1. _____ _____ _____ +

    2. _____ _____ _____ −

    [Mimes *write* to indicate to students that they are to copy question and write two responses, each of three words; the first one expressing positive feelings and the second expressing negative feelings]
    STUDENT: [After some hesitation, looking at their papers and at the teacher, begin writing items like these]

    1. Not too bad. Or: Fine, thank you. Or: Pretty good, thanks.

    2. Very, very tired. Or: Not too good. Or: Bad headache now.

6. TEACHER: [Says the two exchanges below in conversational English. Before saying them, the teacher tells the students to write the exchanges minus the extraneous words or syllables in them. Each exchange is said only once.]

    1. Good nice evening.

STUDENTS: [Some write: 1. Good nice evening; others write: 1. Good evening.]

TEACHER: 2. Fine, thanking you.

STUDENTS: [Some write: 2. Fine thanking you; others write: 2. Fine thank you; still others write: 2. Fine thanks]

JUDGING WAYS OF GREETING STUDENTS

Activity 2

Below I have listed three pairs of judgments I have heard teachers make about teaching practices. Reread the six practices in Activity 1 and write the number of each practice under one of the pairs of judgments.

easy	difficult
boring	less boring
natural	contrived

After class, ask a few students to make their judgments about the activities so you can compare your perspectives and those of your students.

Thinking about the Alternatives

On the blank lines below under *your judgment*, please write in a pair of judgments you want to make about the six ways of greeting students that is different from the three pairs I provided. As you make the judgments, write down the numbers of the practices that you think match the pairs of judgments you made.

Starting Class ■ 131

Then, if possible, ask a colleague to write another pair of judgments. Compare your judgments and the examples you picked.

your judgment

a colleague's judgment

SWITCHING APPROACHES

If you discover that you consistently engage in practices to start class that you judged difficult, less boring, or contrived, do the opposite: Try a practice you normally do not do that you judged easy, boring, or natural for a change, in one or two classes.

If you and your colleague disagreed about what is difficult and easy, each of you can do an opposite and compare judgments again.

Optional Activities: Alternate Perceptions

Activities 2A and 2B under "Starting Class" in the appendix provide other ways to become aware of alternate perceptions.

Activity 3

After you try an opposite way of starting class, write down, on the lines below, your reactions and those of different members of your class to the new practice.

_____
_____
_____
_____
_____
_____
_____
_____
_____

SEEING MULTIPLE EFFECTS

As you stop following the practices you normally follow by trying a number of alternatives, either suggested by others or discovered through observing others, you of course get a clearer idea of the multiple effects of different practices. As you get a clearer idea of relationships between various practices and multiple effects, you may want to generate some alternative practices with a colleague.

One way to generate alternative practices is to describe multiple contrasting characteristics of the practices you and others engage in and do not engage in. Above, you judged practices in many ways: easy or difficult, boring or less boring, and natural or contrived. Now you will match contrasting *descriptions* of each practice, rather than a contrasting *judgment*. A practice from each contrasting description can be selected from the list as a starting point for altering some of the practices you have started to explore.

Activity 4

In the grouping below, I've listed six pairs of contrasting descriptive characteristics. Reread "Ways of Greeting Students," on pages 129–131. Then, under each pair of contrasting descriptive characteristics, write in the number of each practice that you think fits the *descriptive* characteristic.

A. spoken by teacher in classroom intonation	spoken by teacher in conversational intonation
B. spoken by students	written by students
C. single response expected	multiple responses expected
D. no visual clues given	visual clues given
E. students chant or use classroom intonation	students speak with energy, or other emotion
F. response from students requires mainly memory	response from students requires more than memory

Starting Class ■ 133

Thinking about Another Perspective

In the groupings below are my matchings of descriptions with ways of greeting students. If you have a colleague who is interested, invite him or her to match the descriptions and practices separately. Then you can compare yours with more than one perspective.

The advantage of comparing yours with a colleague's is that you can discuss the meanings of the terms as you each use them. The disadvantage of comparing yours with mine is that you might think that mine would be correct. But one of the goals of matching descriptions with practices is to see more clearly what each person means by the descriptive terms. Matching examples of what we mean by a term also shows others what we mean. Consequently, there are no right and wrong matchings. Rather, there are matchings that each makes that reveal to others what each means.

A. spoken by teacher in classroom intonation	spoken by teacher in conversational intonation
1, 2	3, 4, 6

B. spoken by students	written by students
1, 2, 3, 4	5, 6

C. single response expected	multiple responses expected
1, 2	3, 4, 5, 6

D. no visual clues given	visual clues given
1, 2, 6	3, 4, 5

E. students chant or use classroom intonation	students speak with energy, or other emotion
1, 2	3, 4

F. response from students requires mainly memory	response from students requires more than memory
1, 2	3, 4, 5, 6

There are only six pairs of characteristics to describe greeting practices listed here. From your matching and your discussion of that matching you no doubt generated other characteristics of ways of greeting students. So below are blank lines for you to note characteristics of practices that are important to you or to a colleague. Under these labels, from the list of six practices at the beginning of this section, write the appropriate ways of greeting that match the labels you have written on the lines.

               Characteristics   Practices from pages 129–131

G. _____   _____

H. _____   _____

I. _____   _____

J. _____   _____

REACHING OUR GOALS

To generate alternative teaching practices rather than following practices you have observed others follow, the first step is to decide what kinds of practices you want to try, based on judgments you make of the practices you now follow. Judgments are values or beliefs we attribute to what we do. Our judgments reflect the consequences we want from our teaching or the goals we set.

In the usual conversations, judgments are used to stop conversations, to end exploration. In contrasting conversations, judgments are used to open conversations, to begin explorations. Judgments are seen as a way to make our beliefs and values explicit so we can explore them and their relationships to our practices. Judgments are not seen as evaluations.

You have to decide what consequences you want or what goals you want that are different from those you are now seeking. For example, if you judged as difficult Practice 5—the one in which students had to write a positive and a negative three-word reply to "How are you?"—and you think you want to follow a practice that is easy, then you have to make 5 easier. If you or a colleague judged Practice 5 to be contrived, and your goal is to engage in activities that are natural, then you'd have to change Practice 5 to make it more natural.

The next step in making a difficult practice easy or a contrived one natural is to look at the characteristics of the practice as it is. In the case of Practice 5, here are the features I noted on page 133: B. *written by students*; C. *multiple responses expected*; D. *visual clues given*; F. *requires more than memory*.

When we have a few specific characteristics of a practice identified, we can make the practice less difficult by noting features of practices we judged easy, and adding some of these features to the practices we judged difficult. For example, I consider Practice 3 easier than Practice 5. In Prac-

Starting Class ■ 135

tice 3, one of the characteristics I noted was D. *visual clues given*—the sketches of three faces and the first and last letter of each word were both visual clues. Adding letters of some of the words that could be used in writing three-word responses to the blank lines in Practice 5 would make the responses easier in many cases.

One version of Practice 5, with the characteristic of visual clues borrowed from Practice 3, is shown below.

TEACHER: [Writes these items on the blackboard]

How are you?

1. N – – t – – b – – +
   or
   F – – – t – – – – y – – +
   or
   P – – – – – g – – –, t – – – – – +

2. T – – – –, t – – – – y – – –
   or
   N – – t – – g – – – –

[Teacher mimes writing to indicate that students are to copy and complete the responses on the blackboard; teacher holds up two fingers to try to indicate that only two responses are being requested and that students are to select from the options given.]

Activity 5

On the lines below, write a teaching practice that you judged contrived or difficult or as some other characteristic you chose. With a colleague, if possible, add or subtract features from it so that it can be judged the opposite of what it was judged before the changes.

___

On the lines below, write some of your reactions to the process of generating alternative practices for greeting the class.

___

Applications of Observing

Try out the practice you just generated above on the lines below, write your reactions and the reactions of your students to the alternative practice that you tried in class.

___

Thinking about the Alternatives

We realize the multiple results of a number of small events—for lack of a nail, the battle was lost; because of a blowout on one car or a very small patch of ice on one small area of road, hundreds can be affected. These examples, as well as the nature of the changes you were invited to generate in greeting students, illustrate another feature of contrasting conversations: the importance of limiting the size and scope of the alternatives we try. The emphasis in all the sections on specific description, the use of small amounts of data to analyze in a range of ways both imply small changes, of course. But I hope that in this section, in particular, you saw the centrality of avoiding large changes in the exploration of teaching because of the fact that starting class takes up such a small amount of time. The only type of alternatives we can try have to be small.

Small changes—few in number, taking up little time, different from our regular practices in only one or two small features—are likely to be easier to explore. For one thing, a single change can be more thoroughly analyzed in a shorter amount of time than can many changes in the same amount of time. For another, limiting the amount of time during which the change is being tried means the amount of tape we have to analyze is brief enough so as not to seem overwhelming. Aside from making exploration easier, at least in practical ways, the employment of alternatives that are only slight variations of our regular practices probably will limit any extremely distruptive effect.

After you have discussed reactions to various ways of greeting students, you and some students might want to start collecting instances of greetings in a range of settings, as well as in fiction and drama and then discuss their various meanings and effects. The discussion between Brutus and Lucillius in *Julius Caesar* is one of many in literature that illustrates the significance of greetings as well as the need to interpret them in many ways.

> BRUTUS: How did Cassius receive you?
> LUCILLIUS: With courtesy and with respect enough;
> But not with such familiar instances,
> Nor with such free and friendly conference,
> As he hath used of old.
> BRUTUS: Thou hast described
> A hot friend cooling: ever note Lucillius,
> When love begins to sicken and decay.
> It useth an enforced ceremony.
> There are no tricks in plain and simple faith;
> But hollow men, like horses hot at hand,
> Make gallant show and promise of their mettle....
>
> (Act IV, Scene ii)

TAKING STOCK OF OUR GOALS

THE RANGE OF THE THINGS WE DO

If we find some things we do, in a range of settings, that seem to be congruent with some of our goals and if we are able to discover distinctive features of these things, we might be able to apply these features in both our teaching and other aspects of our lives. For example, if we see ourselves and others being challenged by some of the things we do and ask others to do, then we can try to identify the features we think cause the challenge. Then, when our goal requires either challenging or less challenging activities, we can apply the appropriate distinctive features of both types of activities to the tasks at hand.

Obviously, presenting examples of things we do from all possible settings would be overwhelming. Consequently, in this section, I'm going to present things we do and ask others to do from only two settings: a park and a classroom. In both these settings, as in almost all others, there is a mix of things we do and ask others to do that is challenging and less challenging. A park is a public place, usually, like most schools. And, as in schools, a range of age groups can be found in parks. Also, most of us have spent some time both in parks and in classrooms.

Activity 1

Below are listed a number of things we do in classrooms and parks, both on our own and because others ask us to. The first activity is taken from a park near my apartment. It is one block square and is built on two levels, one about twelve feet higher than the other. On the lower level, there is a playing field, and on the upper level there are slides, climbing equipment, and a mound about 20 feet high. Cut in the side of the hill that divides the lower and upper levels is a ramp, which provides access from one level to the other. However, few children use the ramp to get to the swings. They invariably climb up the hill from the lower to the upper level, in spite of the fact that there is a fence at the top of the hill which has been constructed to keep children from climbing the hill separating the two levels. The fence is breached in a number of places. Each spring, park rangers repair the fence and re-sod the hill with grass. They also post a sign saying that the ramp should be used to move from one level to the other, rather than the hill.

At the end of the list of examples is a T with two columns, one titled *challenging* and the other titled *less challenging*. The numbers and key words of some of the things we do in both classrooms and parks that I think are challenging and less challenging, are listed in the appropriate columns. In determining which column they belong in, I looked at the things themselves and, in cases where directions were given that caused the things to be done, at the directions as well. On the blank lines group the activities I did not group in one of the two columns. As you group the examples, you will notice some distinctive features of things we do which contribute towards making them challenging.

Doing Things on Our Own

1. [Children climbing up a steep hill where a sign is located prohibiting climbing, crawling through a small hole in a fence at the top of the hill with friends]

2. [Persons reading crossword puzzle clues and then filling in blank squares in the crossword puzzle]

3. [Two people sitting on a bench talking to each other]

4. [Five children riding unicycles around the park over and over and over again, seeing how long they can continue peddling and balancing]

5. [Two people playing chess on a bench in the park]

6. [One person walking a dog across the street from the park]

7. [A child picks up small pebbles from various places in the park and puts them in her bucket. When she fills the bucket, she dumps it out and then puts the pebbles she just dumped out back in her bucket, being careful to make pebbles just reach the top edge of the bucket.]

8. [A child blowing bubbles]

Doings Things Others Ask Us to Do

9. Why don't you try coming down the hill without holding your handlebars?

9a. [Speeding downhill without holding on to handlebars]

10. Can you give me one type of joint, Aya?

10a. Ball-and-socket joint?

10. [Points to the joint in her index finger and then to the joint in her knee] Carl, which one is the ball-and-socket joint?

10b. The knee.

11. What number goes in the circle? You can use either method— whichever you see first.
$$\frac{6}{3} = \frac{12}{\bigcirc}$$

11a. 6?

12. I have given each of you around a hundred toothpicks and some glue. In pairs, I want you to make a structure with the toothpicks as high as you can that will support this book. You have 30 minutes.

12a. [Two students construct a structure that looks like a log cabin. It cannot support the book and it is only only 1 inch high.]

12b. [Two students make a number of triangles by gluing sets of three toothpicks together. When the glue on these triangles dries, they then glue the triangles together in the shape of a cone. After the cones are dry, they glue one cone to another to produce the structure sketched below. It is strong enough to hold the book, and it is around 10 inches long. They accomplish the task in 30 minutes since the glue is fast-drying.]

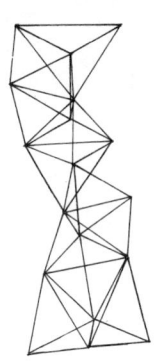

13. Today, we are going to mix yeast and molasses together and a gas will be formed—which we will collect in this tube here.

13a. [As the teacher has been talking, one student who had spilled some granules of dried yeast on his lab table has been carefully brushing the granules into a pile and then with a piece of paper carefully pushes them back into the dried yeast container.]

14. How can we describe *mind*? Smart minds we can say. Reflective minds is also possible. Hidden minds. There are many facets to minds—but what is a facet? It's like a diamond. And what are other characteristics? Open, generous, honest. And then there's reliability—rely on, to trust. They are consistent and we can rely on them. What do you look for in a friend?

14a. [Some people in the room with person speaking look out the window, some have their heads on their arms, some look at the person speaking, some draw sketches on note pads they are holding]

15. Read the first sentence but put the verb at the end of the sentence as you read it.

15a. He toward the exit with the bag of money ran.

16. Shade the boxes on the left to represent .3 and on the right to show .03. Then, let me know whether shading the boxes helped you see that .3 is larger than .03.

16a. [Shades 7 boxes on the left of the large square and part of one on the right]

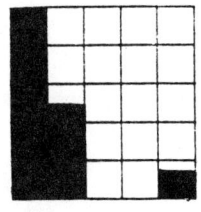

16b. Oh, I see—.3 of 25 is 7.5, but .03 is only .75—part of only 1 box.

Taking Stock of Our Goals ■ 141

Various Groupings

challenging	less challenging
1. climbing hill	3. sitting on bench
2. crossword puzzle	6. walking dog in park
4. riding unicycles	
5. playing chess	
9a. not holding handlebar	

As usual, grouping examples highlights the range of meanings labels can evoke. In trying to decide whether filling a bucket with pebbles (7) is challenging, this question has come up: To be challenging, does something we do have to be difficult in general, or only to the person doing it? The chess players (5) and bubble blower (8) may be enjoying what they are doing. Can we enjoy challenging things we do, or do the things we do have to be serious? If we don't expend much effort—cleaning up yeast granules (13a) burns up fewer calories than racing down a hill on a bicycle (9a)—can the thing we do be challenging? These and other questions led me to group the things we do as shown below. Compare this grouping with your own and that of your partner.

challenging	less challenging
7. picking up pebbles	10a. ball-and-socket joint?
8. blowing bubbles	12a. making a log cabin with toothpicks
11a. 6?	14a. being in class during lecture
12b. toothpick structure that could hold the book	16b. comment on result of shading boxes for math problem
13a. cleaning up yeast	
15a. reading sentence with the verb at the end	
16a. shading boxes for math problem	

Comparing another's grouping with one's own usually raises more questions about the meanings of the labels. Some speculate about conditions that might affect the degree of challenge. For example, if the people play chess (5) very casually, with no care about following the rules, do not keep track of points, nor note the winners, some think they should not be considered doing challenging activities. If the children daily ride unicycles (4) and race down hills without holding on to their handlebars (9a), the degree of challenge might not only decrease, the challenge might disappear. Others speculated about the amount of effort needed. Thus, it becomes hard for some to consider it challenging to pick up pebbles (7) and clean up yeast granules (13a). These activities require hardly any effort, either physical or mental.

*R*E-EXAMINING BELIEFS

Since one aim of this book is to consider all data from a range of perspectives—and as often as possible to turn each grouping upside down or inside out—such speculation is not only welcome but necessary. Indeed, in order to bring to the surface some features that contribute to your beliefs about the meaning of *challenging*, reconsider a few items you entered in each column in the same way you considered some of the items in my columns misplaced. As you do, write down next to the items in the column above a few key words to indicate a reason for moving the item from the column it is in to the opposite column. So, if you entered making a log cabin from toothpicks (12a) in the *less challenging* column, note a reason why it should be placed in the *challenging* column. If you considered walking a dog in the park (6) *less challenging*, give a reason that dog walking might be challenging.

Activity 2

Using the reasons you just generated as well as some I and your partner mentioned, and the examples themselves on the blank lines, in the columns below, write some of the features that you think distinguish challenging and less challenging things we do. Since there are things that involve activity that are both challenging and less challenging, this characteristic does not distinguish the two.

Competition, though, is a characterstic that seems common to at least a few of the challenging things we do and seems absent from the less challenging things we do, so competition is one example of a potentially distinctive feature. I have entered this feature in the challenging column, as an example.

Since a lack of a precise goal seems to be a feature of some of the less challenging things we do, I've entered this feature in the less challenging column. For example, the people on the bench (3) seem to have less precise goals than does the child picking up pebbles (7) and the person cleaning up the yeast granules (13a). In each column write a few more, at least two of which require words that also start with the letter *c*.

distinctive features of challenging things we do	distinctive features of less challenging things we do
competition	lack of a precise goal

Taking Stock of Our Goals ■ 143

In listing the features, we come up with the same types of questions we asked in the initial grouping. Said another way, both activities required us to explore our beliefs about what we consider challenging. Engaging in such exploration is both an admission of ignorance and a proclamation of freedom. The freedom to question, to admit we are not certain. Feynman, the Nobel Prize winner who tries to write about science without jargon, writes about exploration in this way: "The same thrill, the same awe and mystery, comes again and again when we look at any question deeply enough. With more knowledge comes a deeper, more wonderful mystery, luring one to penetrate deeper still . . . we turn over each new stone to find unimagined strangeness leading on to more wonderful questions and mysteries—certainly a grand adventure!" (Feynman, 1988, p. 186)

Here are the words other teachers generated as they turned over the stones, with the c words underlined. In the next section are some illustrations of how the words are related to the examples.

distinctive features of challenging things we do	*distinctive features of less challenging things we do*
competition with others or self is required	lack of a precise goal shared by many
gamelike	no need for any special effort
criteria that are public	require only memory, no type of other thinking skill
choices have to be made in the process of doing the things; sometimes, the choices are made from a range of contrasting possibilities	one can be passive as one does the things
	when one has done the thing, one has to be told by another whether one has done it properly
the person doing the thing knows whether the thing has been done successfully without being told	emphasis is on product—a right answer—rather than on both the process of doing things and on a certain standard of doing the things
require a range of thinking activity beyond memory or recall alone	
the things people are doing on their own or told to do are in some way based on a contrivance	

Thinking about the Grouping

There is, of course, some overlap between the separate features of challenging things we do. And some of the features of things we do that are challenging sometimes apply to a certain extent to things we do that are less challenging. For example, memory is required both for remembering the names of types of joints—ball-and-socket (10a)—and for remembering the rules for playing chess (5). But to play chess, one has to use more than memory, while one can remember the name of a type of joint with memory alone. In the same way, it can be argued that during chess and card games, there are moments when a player can be passive. But any passive moments are juxtaposed with active moments, which is usually less the case when sitting on a bench (3) or walking a dog (6). Of course, if the dog sees a bird, or if those sitting on a bench see an accident, their passive moments are interrupted. But the nature of the activity is not what causes the active moments. Outside incidents cause the active moments and interrupt the passive ones.

As we apply the distinctive features we identify, we see once again that in many cases, some examples of things we do are not absolutely challenging or less challenging. Rather, individual items fit on a continuum in relationship with other items. Thus, the students who make the log cabin with toothpicks (12a) must engage in a greater range of mental activities than does the student who simply has to recall the name for a joint (10a). But since the students who made the log cabins did not discover an alternative design that met the criteria that were publicly established (12), they did not probably engage in as great a range of mental activities as did the students who generated an alternative toothpick design that met the criteria (12b).

Likewise, it can be argued that whenever another person tells us to do something, that person has contrived to get us to do something. But the ingenuity required is greater in doing some things others tell us to do than in doing others. These things seem to require more contrivance, rather than less: constructing and completing a crossword puzzle (2), developing the rules of chess and playing the game (5), inventing the criteria for the toothpick structure and constructing it (12 and 12b), planning the unnatural reading task that required reading with a verb in a new position (15a) and designing a drawing (16) to illustrate the difference between decimal places (16a). These activities required less contrivance than the ones just noted: walking a dog (6) and listening to others talk about yeast (13) or the mind (14). One reason that I have listed both the thing that was done as well as the direction given to get the thing done in many of these examples of contrived things is that the contrivance is often in the directions given or the rules previously developed and learned rather than in the performance of the thing itself.

Once we make explicit some of the features we think distinguish challenging from less challenging things, we can reconsider some of our original choices. If we determine that challenging things must exhibit each and every one of the distinctive features we list, the number of items grouped as challenging might decrease. For example, though determining which body joints are ball-and-socket joints (10b) may require more mental activity than the memory alone required by remembering one type of joint (10a), for the person saying that the knee is a ball-and-socket joint but the finger joint is not, there are no criteria to use in knowing whether the correct response has been given; the criteria are not public. Nor is the question or answer about joints gamelike.

In addition, there is a lack of a precise goal that is *shared by many*. While some other students may know what the teacher expects, based on a previous lesson, it is the teacher who determines whether the answer given is the right one. So the goal is precise, but the precise goal is not shared by many in the same way that the goal is shared by those unlawfully climbing the hill in the park (1), riding unicycles (4), playing chess (5), racing down the hill (9a), building a toothpick structure to meet publicly stated criteria (12b), or reading sentences with the verb at the end (15a).

Thinking about the Alternatives

Whether your distinctive features and the ones I have listed are similar or different is, of course, not important. Nor should any consternation result if we each consider different things we do challenging or less challenging. What *is* important is first that we make explicit what we consider challenging and less challenging, or involving and less involving, or relevant and less relevant, or whatever other judgments we want to explore.

Then, it is important to try to see how what we consider challenging, relevant, or involving can in fact be the opposite—less challenging, less relevant, or less involving.

Next, we need to list features of communications we have determined are examples of each group. We then have to apply these distinctive features to the original examples. As we apply the distinctive features, we often decide to move some of our examples from one grouping to another.

Finally, if we are interested in changing the proportion of communications that fit in both of the groupings we have established so that they are more congruent with our goals, we have to play with the characteristics. We have to add some characteristics to those communications that do not have them and delete them from those that do. There are two steps to this final part of the game: First, we have to manipulate the features on paper; second, we have to try the newly generated communications in actual interaction with others.

If we agreed that the announcement about yeast and molasses (13) belonged in the *less challenging* column, and we had decided our goal was to have more challenging activities, then the next step would be to note which features were absent. First, there is no goal at all, either precise or general. No effort is needed on the part of the students and they are passive. The lack of any student effort required is supported by the fact that one student, at least, is able to concentrate intently on returning the yeast granules to the container from which they spilled (13a). If the student had been required to do something, the student could not concentrate on cleaning up the granules. No contrivance is present in the teacher's words. If we wanted to add these features, the teacher's communication might look like this:

1. "As I start to explain today's lesson,
2. write down the following:
3. names of each solid I mention,
4. names of each liquid I mention,
5. each word which begins with the letter g.
6. You should have eight items on your sheet by the time my explanation is over."

7. [Teacher writes *solid* above one column on the blackboard and *liquid* above another; in a separate column, she writes the letter g three times, like this:]

8. g ——————— g ——————— g ———————

The directions in line 6 state a precise goal. Each student should have eight items written. To meet this goal, some criteria are mentioned in lines 3, 4, and 5. And the criteria are made slightly more explicit in lines 7 and 8. It can even be argued that by writing the "rules" that the students are expected to play by, a gamelike spirit is introduced that is similar to that of kids when they decide to climb a hill and breach a fence (1), when some bicycle riders tell others to try riding without holding the handlebars (9), and that is present in the completion of a crossword puzzle (2) and when playing chess (5). Said another way, the distinctive features are interrelated and overlap in such a way that adding one often results in the generation of one or two related ones. Contrivance, after all, is a feature that can lead to a gamelike spirit. Games, it can be argued, are symbols of contrivance, since they are unnatural activities. Sitting on a bench requires no invention; sitting on a bench playing chess requires invention. Walking a dog requires less invention than riding a unicycle. And riding a unicycle requires less invention than a game such as baseball or basketball.

When you were asked to list at least two distinctive features of challenging and less challenging things we do that begin with the letter *c*, this additional criterion could be considered a contrivance. Because you had to match words you generated against this criterion, you were required to engage in one additional mental activity.

At the same time, the criterion helps you see whether you are successful or not. If you come up with no words that begin with the letter *c*, then you know you have not been completely successful, even if you have listed a dozen distinctive features. Since the criterion is public, though, you can see whether your partner has met the criterion. Comparing your responses on the basis of this criterion also might add a bit of competition, another distinctive feature of challenging things we do. Since the criterion makes the goal a bit more precise, may require a bit more specific effort, forces us to move beyond memory alone, and does not allow us to remain passive, we can see that many of the features of less challenging things we do are not met. So, again, we see evidence that one small change of one feature can affect other features. We can see that the differences between challenging and less challenging in things we do can be quite small. And that making things we do challenging or less challenging does not necessarily require large changes. Learning how to look at things we do differently does not require large changes either, only a series of quite small changes.

WAYS OF NOTING RELATIONSHIPS BETWEEN DIFFERENT TYPES OF COMMUNICATIONS

Throughout this book, much that we have explored has consisted of rather obvious things, things that we often take for granted and thus do not notice. Or, if we do notice them, we do not consider them important. The mystery writer Simenon often has his main character, Inspector Maigret, reflect on this phenomenon of failing to notice small, everyday communications of one sort or another. During one investigation, Simenon has Inspector Maigret share this reflection: "The most frustrating cases are those that seem so run-of-the-mill that at first you don't think they're important. It's like those illnesses that sneak up on you, beginning with vague discomfort. When you finally take them seriously, it's often too late." (Simenon, 1974, p. 1)

One of the obvious things we all know is the fact that we communicate with our facial expressions, our clothing, our gestures, our tone of voice, through sketches—to name a few—as well as through spoken or written words. Yet we often fail to take notice of this fact or, if we do make a comment such as "his tone of voice sounded skeptical to me," we often fail to explore the relationships between, say, tone of voice and other means of communicating along with tone of voice. This section is devoted to communications we often fail to take notice of—and therefore fail to consciously alter—and relationships between different types of communications.

A NEW LOOK AT HOW WE COMMUNICATE

In the course of any day we write our names many times. Suppose we had to communicate a name to someone who did not use the convenience of spelling. We could act it out or illustrate the sounds. Below is a sketch of my own first and last names to try to illustrate the idea:

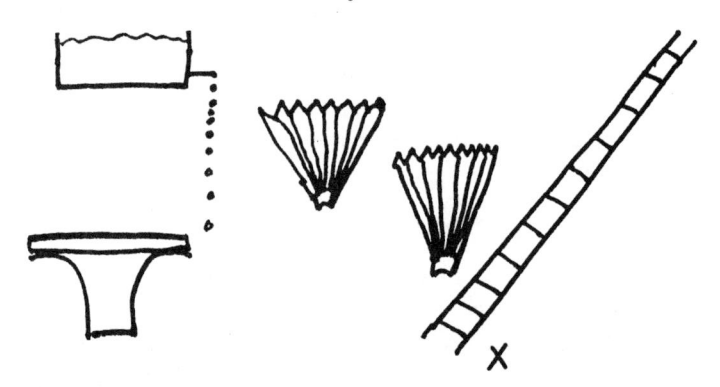

The goals of sketching are twofold: (1) to see means we use to communicate in addition to words; (2) to see relationships between these different means we use to communicate. While trying to discover the relationships between the sketches and the names they represent, we also see the meanings that features in the sketch have to another person, and we see the types of questions we use to discover meanings.

Activity 1

When you are together with your partner, individually select a person you both know and sketch some pictures to represent the first and last names of that person. Do your sketching in the space below while your partner draws on another sheet of paper. Do not, of course, reveal the identity of the person whose names you are sketching. If you are left-handed, try sketching with the pencil or pen held in the right hand, and vice versa. You or your partner may not want to play the game, preferring to use your usual hand. Using the opposite hand, though, may enable you to realize something you did not realize before, one of the aims of this book, as of any learning.

When the sketches are completed and guessing begins, questions will be allowed. But please hold the questions until after the sketches are finished. As the sketches are being drawn, start a tape recorder to determine whether any sounds or comments are made during the sketching. During the next activity, you will be listening to the tape.

When the sketches representing two names are finished, you have to identify the name for your partner's sketch, and your partner has to identify the name in your sketch. As the questions begin, try to tape-record the exchange. After you each discover the identity of the person sketched, you will listen to the recording. If you do not have access to a tape recorder, stop every few questions and jot down in the space below the sounds either of you are making as you ask and respond to the questions.

In either case, with or without tape-recording, jot down descriptions of some of the gestures, facial expressions, or movements you each used as you were asking and answering questions. Or draw some stick figures showing gestures and movements.

Only yes-no questions are allowed. So, in the case of the pictures representing my name, the question "Is that water dripping in the first sketch?" is acceptable while "What is the first sketch a picture of?" or "Why is there an x at the bottom of the picture?" is not.

Since you may not have any idea whose name was sketched, you may ask questions to narrow down the possibilities, but these too must be yes-no questions only, such as "Is it the name of a person we know at school?" In short, this is a variety of the game "Twenty Questions."

Activity 2

If you had the recorder going during the sketching, listen to the tape now and write down below anything you hear on the tape other than words. You can write either sounds themselves or descriptions of them. But do not write down any words that were spoken.

If you did not tape-record, write down from memory things you heard other than words. In subsequent activities in this section, you will be asked to group the various means of communicating other than words.

During sketching
_____
_____
_____
_____

Sounds heard as yes/no questions were asked and answered
_____
_____
_____
_____

Gestures and movements observed as yes/no questions were asked and answered
_____
_____
_____
_____

150 ■ Applications of Observing

Sketches of gestures, expressions, movements

Activity 3

In order to note relationships between the different means used to communicate during the sketching and the asking of questions about the sketches, I suggest that you rewrite what you have already written down, but in a new way.

Below, write sounds and other means together. For example, if you said, "Huh?" I'd like you to describe other sounds or gestures that seemed to accompany "Huh?" In other words, I would like you to write what you heard and what you saw in relationship to each other.

While it might have been easier to write all the means used together, by inviting you to write them separately first and then combining them now I hope to highlight the importance of the relationships between the different means we use to communicate. On many checklists used to observe teachers, the means we use to communicate are in fact noted separately. For example, an evaluation form might ask a supervisor to note the teacher's use of eye contact on one line, the teacher's use of tone of voice on another, instances of silence on still another.

Note that the space below does not contain any lines so that you can draw sketches under sounds if you wish; you are not limited to writing words to describe words and other means used to communicate.

Thinking about Relationships

Here are some sounds, gestures, facial expressions, and so forth that seemed to accompany each other during the sketching and asking of yes/no questions about the sketches, as observed by others:

> While drawing lines, my partner nodded his head and said "yup."
>
> After finishing one part of the sketch, my partner put one hand on his chin, looked at the partial sketch, and let air out of his mouth that made a faint hissing sound.
>
> While I asked some questions about the sketch, my partner kept crossing and uncrossing his legs and kept shaking his head sideways.
>
> As I asked some questions, I put my finger on the sketch and pointed to the part of the sketch that I was asking about.
>
> As I said, "Oh, I know what that stands for-it's a toilet-a john," I raised my voice and tapped my index finger on the sketch of the "john."
>
> When I finally guessed the connection between the sketches and the names of the person my partner had sketched, I laughed and shook my partner's hand, at about the same time.

The types of relationships we have been dealing with are discussed by Bateson. Writing of the mental process, he reminds us that defining a stem and a leaf separately is almost impossible:

> The correct units of description are not leaf and stem but the relations between them. . . .
> In the same way, most of us were taught in school that a noun is the name of a person, place, or thing, but what we should have been taught is that a noun can stand in various kinds of relationship to other parts of the sentence, so that the whole of grammar could be defined as relationship and not in terms of things.
>
> (Bateson & Bateson, 1988, pp. 27, 28)

DIFFERENT MAPS OF REALITY

Some forms used by supervisors to observe teachers not only separate different means teachers use to communicate, having separate entries for eye contact, movement, tone of voice, and silence, but they also imply that the features on the form are worth noting. The statement that Korzybski is perhaps most famous for—"the map is not the territory"—reminds us that neither the items on evaluation forms nor the items you and I and your partner noted represent *Reality*.

Rather, each simply produces a different map of reality in the same way that different government organizations each prepare maps to reveal the features of an area they are concerned with. Thus, the police develop maps which show the location of police stations and incidence of different types of crime. The tax office creates maps which show the different types of real estate and the values of each. The post office authorities must map out routes for delivering mail; the parks department has to keep track of where trees are planted, where parks are located, and so forth. While each map is important to each separate office, failing to compare maps prevents each group from seeing relationships between the variable each is in charge of. If the police looked at the tax office map, they might see relationships between theft and value of houses. If the parks department and police compared crime rates to the locations of different types and sizes of parks, they might see ways to decrease crime in some parks. (Bateson, 1972, pp. 449, 453)

Activity 4

In order to see the relationships between the different means we use to communicate as well as to see multiple characteristics of these different means, group the communications you wrote in previous activities below.

As you can see, there are four pairs of columns. Reread the examples of media, of means of communication, which were used together in Activity 3—either your examples or those observed by others. Then take some of these examples and group them in at least three ways in the columns provided. Write titles above each column to note the features of the communications you are noting in each grouping.

For example, one set of pairs might be *heard and seen/seen and felt*. Another could be *unconnected to task/connected to task*.

Ways of Noting Relationships ■ 153

Way 1 _____|_____   Way 2 _____|_____

|
|
|
|
|
|

Way 3 _____|_____   Way 4 _____|_____

|
|
|
|
|
|

Thinking about the Alternatives

Here are some titles others generated both to highlight relationships between the means we use to communicate and to group, or characterize, the means we use to communicate:

- heard and seen/seen and felt
- required for getting the meaning across/not required to get the meaning across
- signs of being nervous/other
- showing us connecting/showing us being separate
- unconnected to task/connected to task
- emotional/unemotional
- genuine/not genuine
- Hollywood/not Hollywood

Almost all of us point to something we are referring to with words. Look again at the sketch I made of my name. Someone might ask: "Is the ladder there (touching the sketch of the ladder with his or her right index finger) to show high and low?" Since there is only one ladder in the sketch, the finger does not add any information; it seems *not required to get the meaning across*. Yet we point as we speak and as we alter our intonation. When I have sketched pictures for my names on a blackboard

154 ■ Applications of Observing

in large classrooms, people point toward the ladder or toward the chain hanging from the water container above the toilet bowl, even when I am looking at the blackboard and therefore cannot see their fingers. They often seem to look back and forth between the sketch on the blackboard and a person sitting close to them as they point, also.

I have found myself adjusting my tie while speaking on the phone though obviously the person cannot see my appearance nor has the topic been ties or even dress. As I adjust my tie, I often seem to change my tone of voice at the same time.

Some copied the same gestures that they had at first written under the heading *not required to get the meaning across* under the headings *showing us connecting, emotional,* and *genuine*. These gestures were at times accompanied by some "uhs," and so the "uhs" were placed in many columns at the same time.

Activity 5

Observe a class or a videotape of a class for a short time, with *short* meaning around 3 minutes. Write down some means other than words students use to communicate. Then either think back on the class you observed live or replay the videotape and write some other means used by the students to communicate. Keep replaying or rethinking until you have at least three examples.

_____
_____
_____
_____

Go back to the grouping you just did in Activity 4 and see whether any of the examples you noted while watching students fit any of the categories you established in the columns there. If some examples fit some categories, copy the examples in the appropriate column in Activity 4. Underline them to distinguish them from the ones you had previously written, those collected from the sketching and questioning activity.

Below, write the examples that do *not* seem to fit the categories you established in Activity 4. As before, there are four pairs, though you may need only one or two to note additional features.

Way 1 _____|_____   Way 2 _____|_____

Way 3 _____|_____   Way 4 _____|_____

Ways of Noting Relationships ■ 155

Thinking about the Alternatives

After observing students, some observers report that the means students use to communicate with the teacher other than words are few, or are hard to see, at least. But between students, they find many instances. Under the heading *showing us connecting* few entries are made in many classrooms between teacher and students, but many are made between students. In the sketching and questioning about sketching activities, there were many instances of communications that fit these labels, among some partners. Perhaps there were many examples because in these activities, both you and your partner were relating to each other as peers—the same way students often relate to each other.

Some student-to-student communications fit under previous titles. For example, when students whispered to each other, they often put their hand over their mouth, lowered their heads, and turned sideways as well as lowering their voices. These examples fit *heard and seen, signs of being nervous, showing us connecting,* and *unconnected to task.* When students wanted to answer a question, they not only raised their hands but they tended to look toward the teacher, raise themselves in their chairs, and often blink their eyes. These movements fit under *seen and felt* and *Hollywood.*

But since many of the communications observed seemed to be from student to student rather than from student to teacher, some added the heading *someone in charge/to a peer* in the above grouping. Since many of the responses were to questions the teacher knew the answer to or that required students to try to figure out what the teacher wanted them to say, these categories were added as well: *responding to questions the person asking knows the answer to/responding to questions that seek information.*

Below are listed some relationships between mediums that other people put under the new titles. If you see places where some of the examples you wrote in your notes fit, copy the examples down under the appropriate columns. Noting ways *students* communicate might provide some insight into ways *we* communicate with peers in juxtaposition to someone in charge, and when we respond to questions in order to share information in juxtaposition to showing another we know something.

to someone in charge	to a peer
holds hands tightly	moves hands during speaking
uses words alone	uses words and pauses—ah, markers—uh, fillers—uhm
does not seem to move legs	moves legs a bit

156 ■ Applications of Observing

responding to questions the person asking knows the answer to	responding to questions that seek information
holds hands tightly	moves hands during speaking
uses words	uses words and pauses—ah, markers—uh, fillers—uhm
seems to keep head straight	moves head by tilting it

Some people who borrowed the *Hollywood/not Hollywood* headings that some had written in the first grouping put *responding to questions the person asking knows the answer to* under *Hollywood* because Hollywood connoted insincerity to them. Others put the same questions under *not Hollywood* because to them Hollywood connoted acting. Acting involves using one's body, pausing, moving—not just uttering words.

Activity 6

Without your partner, list below some disadvantages of using words alone or arranging classes so students tend to use words alone. Realize though that using words alone is probably impossible in a class setting. But, in some communications the use of words together with other means of communicating seems easier to notice. Next, list some disadvantages of using words plus other means to communicate.

Disadvantages of words alone
_____
_____
_____
_____
_____
_____

Disadvantages of words and other means
_____
_____
_____
_____
_____
_____

Ways of Noting Relationships

Thinking about the Alternatives

From time to time, most of us come upon a teaching practice that we believe is extremely valuable or a waste of time. Whenever we see an instance of the practice, we tend to think of still another advantage or disadvantage of the practice. Such behavior is not unusual—as Simenon, among others, has pointed out. Here again we have Simenon reminding us of this behavior through Inspector Maigret: "He [Inspector Maigret] was only too familiar with the state of mind he had been in for the last few hours.... It was the feeling that he's made a mistake, that everything was wrong.... That's how it always was. If he felt he was getting into a mess, he became so determined to prove himself right that he waded in all the deeper." (Simenon, 1940, p. 87)

To prevent "wading in all the deeper," on the same lines where you wrote the disadvantages, rewrite two or three of the disadvantages to show how each could be considered an advantage. Then compare them both with your partner's rewrites and with what others wrote below:

> Letting students pause can be a disadvantage because quicker students might get impatient. While quicker students might get impatient, if others are not given time, they might not participate so much.
>
> Having students use their bodies as they speak and perhaps alter their tone of voice could lead to disruption of the class. The teacher might not be able to keep the class under control.
>
> Having the students using more than words might lead to fewer attempts on the part of the students to break the silence since they might have less of a need to speak out of turn if they feel they are speaking in what they consider a meaningful way during the time when speaking is going on.

RELATING CLASSROOM COMMUNICATION TO THE OUTSIDE WORLD

Activity 7

Observe relationships between different means of communications outside of classrooms. Note some of the relationships you observe below. For example, when you are in a bank, observe two tellers and the ways they interact with different customers. Then observe the ways the tellers interact with each other. Or, watch a bus driver and the passengers interact as they get on or off the bus. If you see a coach with a team on a ball field, note some of the ways the coach and the players connect and do not connect with each other with means other than words.

Sounds and gestures outside of classrooms

_____

_____

_____

_____

Select some observations you made and try to fit them into some of the pairs of titles you used to group relationships between mediums. Compare the relationships between mediums when people outside of classrooms communicate with the relationships between them inside of classrooms when students communicate.

Speculate about relationships between the different means we use to communicate and the types of tasks each person is setting for the other. Also, consider the relationships between roles and the means used. Who is in charge, if anyone? Who is providing help or advice or knowledge? When are fewer and more means to communicate used?

As you continue to explore relationships between the different means we use to communicate, you might begin to wonder how much the ways we act are related to each unique personality and how much are related to ways of acting that seem to occur no matter what the personality.

In writing about communication in classrooms, Barnes discussed the tension between the claim that patterns in each of our classrooms are unique and the claim that there are patterns such as relationships between different means used to communicate that were common in many classrooms.

> [Suggesting to teachers that] there are patterns in their classroom behaviour which can be described and compared with that of other teachers or with their own on another occasion [is a recipe for unpopularity because teachers] believe that their teaching is a unique response to what their pupils say and do, arising moment by moment during lessons. . . . There is, however, much evidence to show that there are common patterns in teaching behaviour, and that some of these can be generalized across different levels of education and even from country to country, if we confine ourselves to highly industrialized nations.
>
> (Barnes, 1976, p. 172)

The activities in this section, as in the other sections, have, I hope, reminded you of the strength of both claims Barnes discusses. And perhaps the activities have also reminded you that in exploring teaching, as in much of life, "right" answers can stop exploration. The social worker Saul Alinsky, quoting Leonard Hand, an American federal judge, reminded us that exploration is not just something that applies to our teaching:

> The mark of a free [person] is that ever-gnawing inner uncertainty as to whether or not [one] is right. The consequence is that [one] is ever on the hunt for the cause of [our] plight and the general propositions that help to make some sense out of [our] irrational world. [One] must constantly examine life, including [our] own, to get some idea of what it is all about, and [one] must challenge and test [one's] own findings. Irreverence, essential to questioning, is a requisite. Curiosity becomes compulsive. [Our]

most frequent word is "Why?" What is a question mark but an inverted plow, breaking up the hard soil of old beliefs and preparing for the new growth?

(Alinsky, 1971, p. 11)

And Shakespeare reminded us of how doubts can stifle our actions:

LUCIO: Our doubts are traitors
And make us lose the good we oft might win
By fearing to attempt.

(*Measure for Measure*, Act I, Scene iv)

APPENDIX

Optional Activities

PART ONE

THE GROUPING PROCESS

Activity 2A: Additional Practice with the Grouping Process

When Walt Whitman wrote "Not I, not any one else can travel that road for you, / you must travel it for yourself," I think he realized that travel and exploration include the chance to try a lot of different roads, and even the chance to get off the road for awhile to take shortcuts and to rest.

For those of you who are intrigued by looking for different features on the stamps, move each of the stamps either visually or tactilely from column to column in the groupings below. See whether you can find the feature named in the column title represented on the stamp.

As before, there are some right answers here, with *right* meaning examples that fit the titles of the columns—not that the titles are *right* or *good* or more imaginative or less imaginative than yours. Again, I've left two columns blank so that as you and your partner match stamps and labels and see new characteristics, different from the ones called for, you can feel free to note them, if you wish.

1. *phallic symbols* 2. *flying things*

3. *wood* 4. *commemoration of exploration*

5. *your title* 6. *a colleague's title*

Thinking about the Alternatives

Here are matchings done by others of labels and stamps:

1. *Phallic symbols.* The zeppelin (#3) is the stamp that produced this category in the first place. Old Faithful in Yellowstone (#6) is considered by many to fit in the same category. The staff of the flag in the 5-cent Fremont (#8) is seen as identical with any other "staff." Though some have argued that the timber mast in the center of the hold in the hull of the *Mayflower* (#13) is just like a flagpole, often they are convinced that they are carrying the argument too far.

2. *Flying things.* At first this lens seems to show nothing one cannot see at a glance. Lindbergh's plane (#1), the zeppelin (#3), and the *Curtiss Jenny* (#12) are the only things that fly! But then, often when each stamp is put under the column, a person notices that the discus about to be thrown by the discus thrower (#7) could be considered a flying thing. The water from Old Faithful (#6) surely flies away? And what of the clouds above the Rocky Mountains (#8)? Could there have been insects in the hold of the *Mayflower* (#13)? An absurd notion! Yet by looking again and again, like the detectives in mystery stories, might we find just the insight or piece of evidence we need to turn our entire view of reality around? To see something we did not previously see and thus to learn?

3. *Wood.* The wood that comprises the hulls of the *Santa Maria* (#4) and the *Mayflower* (#13) are immediately put under the wood category by many, along with the biplane in the 24-cent stamp (#12). Lindbergh's *Spirit of St. Louis* (#1) is not immediately listed here, but when those doing the sorting think back, after having included it, they argue that the plane must have had some wood in it also. The flagpole in the 5-cent Fremont (#8) was probably made of wood. The trees on the mountains are, of course, also wood. Are the flags in the 5-cent Lincoln (#5) on wooden staffs?

4. *Commemoration of exploration.* Lindbergh (#1), Byrd (#2), Count Zeppelin's air ships (#3), Columbus (#4), Fremont (#8)—all are really symbols of exploration. But what of Lincoln (#5)? He was looking for new ways for people to live together, without slaves. What of Pocahontas (#9)? She died in England, which is the stage in her life depicted on the stamp. She no doubt was as keen to learn new things as those who came and found her in what they called Jamestown. Were not the pilgrims signing the compact (#13) explorers? They were seeking a new way of life. What of those who go to the Olympic Games every four years, commemorated in Myron's Discobolus on a 5-cent U.S. stamp (#7)? Are they not exploring how far they can push their endurance and their energy? Were those who designed the Curtiss Jenny biplane (#12) not explorers of air travel as much as Columbus was an explorer of a new route to India?

And are you then not an explorer, too? Only if we accept Bronowski's claim: "the discoveries of science, the works of art are explorations ... of a hidden likeness.... In science and in art and in self-knowledge we explore and move constantly by turning to the world of sense to ask, Is this so? This is the habit of truth, always minute yet always urgent." (Bronowski, 1956, pp. 19, 43)

5 and 6. *Your Title and Your Colleague's Title.* The range of titles people come up with is of course very diverse. But the words *ugly* and

beautiful or *attractive* and *unattractive* come up in many sorting conversations. Comparable words—*exciting, engaging, boring, uninteresting*—come up in conversations about lessons. One purpose of the activities in this book is to remind you of ways that you can use such judgments to explore the values you and another person hold rather than to evaluate the lesson.

RECONSTRUCTING OBSERVED LESSONS

Activity 10A: Using Facts

With a partner, put in the columns below the thirteen lines from Activity 10 on pages 31 and 32 that fit under one of the two descriptors on the top of each column. And put the additional lines in brackets in the appropriate columns as well, along with the brackets, so the original lines can be distinguished from the additions. If some lines fit neither column, write them on the blank lines below the columns, after the label "Neutral." After you finish, compare your groupings with the ones printed below.

transcription or narrative details to describe	*transcription or narrative details used to support judgments and interpretations*

Neutral

_____
_____
_____
_____
_____
_____
_____

Neither you nor your partner could help but notice that sometimes the facts that were added produced an interpretation (2 and 5), sometimes they supported an interpretation (6 and 9), and sometimes the facts that

Part One ■ 163

were added contradicted the notes (7, 8, and 10). And some lines did neither, or were netural (1).

CONVERSATIONS ABOUT TEACHING: A REVIEW

Activity 15A: Drawing Images

In the Introduction, I used the image of a magnifying glass to illustrate one feature of the usual conversations and that of a magnifying glass plus a mirror to illustrate one feature of contrasting conversations. In the space below, draw some images that illustrate for you some of the features of each type of conversation. When you finish, ask a person you have been working with to write a u c or a c c next to each image. Then compare the labels with your intentions for each image that you sketched.

164 ■ Optional Activities

Here are images others drew:

Activity 16A: Additional Implications

Here is a transcription from a discussion some teachers had after reading the "Introduction" and "Part One" of this book. It contains some statements and implications in common with those I listed and some that are slightly different. As you can see, I have left some words out. Read the transcribed comments, filling in the blanks. This activity shows us the many ways statements and implications can be phrased—and thus is a review of what we have explored together so far.

Part One ■ 165

The point for me is that you don't know what _____ (1) and what doesn't work—getting away from the old model of observation where people have decided what _____ (2). That's why we have blackboards, chalk, and chairs. Now, they've decided what works is _____ (3). And the momentum of deciding what works, what is _____ (4) teaching is so strong; but the point is we don't know if that student sitting there who is quiet is _____ (5) or not—all we can know is that the student is quiet. The point is to suspend for one moment our idea of _____ (6) teaching and _____ (7) teaching which come from the books and are part of the machine. The point is to say "Oh, what's going on?" and not engage in that _____ (8), but tape or sketch and limit our time after we get a sample of teaching to talk about what you saw and then what I _____ (9) and then we both might _____ (10) something we never saw before—not in the books and not in the good teaching and bad teaching prejudices. The whole point is as teachers we want _____ (11). And we can't get choices if we're saying "That's a mistake" because that means I'm never going to do it again. If you say speaking _____ (12) is what I'll do or speaking fast is what I'll do, you aren't using choices. But if you do both and compare consequences you are using choices. "What works?" is the _____ (13) approach we may be addicted to. I think the point is that the products—the suggestions and the alternatives—are not as _____ (14) as the process, the steps for observing and discussing the excerpts. We are supposed to write down what we observe—not our feelings. In the usual way, there is an underlying _____ (15) that the observer knows more and is passing on _____ (16).

Thinking about the Alternatives

Here are the words that were said in the original discussion, together with some alternatives others wrote in as they read the transcription. Consequently, if you wish, you can compare your words with those of others—not so you can check to see if you got the "right" answers, but to see what ideas came to your mind in comparison to what ideas came to the minds of others.

1. *works*
2. *works* was the word said in both lines but other words could be used, such as *succeeds*
3. *groups* was the word in the original, but the name for any method or technique could be used: *higher order questioning, modulated reinforcement, process approach, emphasis on the affective domain,* and so on
4. *good* was the word in the original, but *superior, outstanding, excellent, prized,* or any other positive adjective is possible
5. *learning* was in the original, but *paying attention, daydreaming,*

or any other words that would attempt to describe what a quiet student might be doing could fit

6. *good*
7. *bad*
8. *judging*
9. *saw*
10. *discover* was used, but *see* or *find* are of course possible here, just as synonyms are possible in 6 through 9
11. *choices* was used but *alternatives* and *options* also fit
12. *slowly* is the word used and since it is matched by *fast* later in the sentence, it is not easy to substitute another word, but the pair *slowly/fast* could be replaced by *with energy/without energy*, *with condescension/without condescension*, or any other pairs that can be used to describe various ways we speak
13. *product*
14. *important* was used but *significant* is possible, of course, as are *critical*, *vital*, and so forth
15. *assumption* was used but other words could have been said including *belief* or *stance*
16. *knowledge* was said but *experience*, *ideas*, *insights*, *methods* all fit

PART TWO

COMMUNICATIONS WITHOUT LANGUAGE

Activity 8A: Clothes as Body Language

The incident between the blind man and the policemen reminded us that clothing is a part of body language, or at least nonlanguage data that we use in attributing motives and beliefs to others. Had the blind man been able to see the uniforms of those who asked him to empty his pockets, his subsequent behavior might have been different. That clothes tell others about us and that we use the clothes of others to determine what we think and feel about them is not news of course. What may be news is the importance placed on clothes in many aspects of school life. When some students are asked what happened at school at the end of the day, they respond by describing what the teacher wore or what some classmates wore more frequently than by describing anything they learned. In some schools that have dress codes; some administrators and teachers devote as much attention to what students wear as to what they study or how they are taught. Commands that deal with clothing—"Take your hat off," for example—are as common in some schools as commands to study.

In order to see ways our perceptions of clothes as a part of body language affect how we deal with others, write in the columns below four contrasting perceptions of why students might wear hats inside a school in spite of the fact that there is a school regulation that prohibits the wearing of hats. (*Hats* of course is simply a metaphor for any forbidden or sought-after bit of clothing or adornment that can be considered a part of body language. In some places makeup, earrings, short skirts, or trousers made from certain materials are forbidden; in some places head scarves, ties, pins, school hats, blazers, or jackets are required.)

Optional Activities

Here are some perceptions about wearing hats in school buildings, as noted by others:

defy authority	show respect for authority
attract attention	deflect attention
be stylish	be unstylish
unconscious habit	planned statement
keep head warm	keep "cool"
like colors of cloth	don't like color of hair

The incident between the policemen and the blind man would no doubt have developed differently had the uniforms been visible. Just as we are likely to resist a person who comes up to us and demands we empty our pockets if we cannot see the type of clothes the person is wearing, so we are likely to treat people according to what we attribute to be the reason for their wearing or not wearing particular clothes. Some of our behavior is based on how we perceive the motives of others. Consequently, if we attribute the wearing of a hat to being stylish, we will try to discourage hat wearing by some admonitions related to style. If we think a person is wearing a hat to defy us, we will perhaps consider punishments to firm up our authority.

In order to see how our solutions to what we perceive as problems are related, write down something you would say or do if you perceived hat wearing in a particular way. Below each perception of why a student is wearing a hat in a place where it is prohibited, write down something you would likely say or do that you think matches your perception of the reason for wearing the hat. Assume the role of a teacher in doing the activity.

Defy authority

_____
_____
_____
_____

Show respect

_____
_____
_____
_____

Unconscious habit

_____
_____
_____
_____

Planned statement

_____
_____
_____
_____

Thinking about the Possibilities

Here are some comments others made about the perceptions of why students were wearing hats:

> Defy Authority:
>
> Why do you have your hat on? You know there is a rule against wearing hats!
>
> I'd pick the hat off the student's head and have it locked in the office, call the parents and tell them they would have to come to pick it up and discuss the matter with me.
>
> Why not photograph the student with the hat on in the hall and send it to the parents or use it in a meeting with the principal?
>
> Unconscious Habit:
>
> Remember, hats off in school; just like no smoking. We all forget to do something we aren't used to.
>
> I'd wear a hat and when I saw a student passing in the hall, I would point to my hat to remind them that they forgot to take theirs off. I'd smile as I did it; no reason to get angry and upset.

If you have been assuming that people who wear particular clothes and move in particular ways are weird, stupid, guilty, or uninterested in learning, consider how such people could in fact be the opposite of what you think they are. Try to assume innocence rather than attributing guilt to those you have determined to be guilty. If, on the other hand, you have been assuming that other groups who wear other types of clothing and move in other ways are normal, clever, innocent, or interested in learning, consider how such people could in fact be the opposite of what you think they are. Try to assume guilt rather than attributing innocence to those you have determined to be innocent. As we look through contrasting frames or glasses, if nothing else we notice that our frames tend to be absolute. We notice also that the perceived characteristic itself fails to reflect the complexity of intentions, motivations, and actions present.

FEEDBACK

Activity 3A: Applying Others' Characteristics

Below are features other people generated in Activity 3 on page 76 and 77. Copy as many characteristics of feedback as apply on the blank lines under each instance of feedback below that was provided during the reading lesson. As you copy more than one characteristic on a line, you will see multiple characteristics or features on the lines, as I have shown for line 1. These multiple characteristics remind us of the limitation of one-dimensional comments about feedback—such as "You should be more explicit," or "You need to be positive," or "Don't give negative feedback."

Other people's characteristics of feedback:

words alone	nonwords or words plus		negative or positive	information

shows teacher in charge	does not show anyone in charge		specifies error	does not specify error

implicit information	explicit information		discouraging	encouraging

appeal to the eye	appeal to other senses		emotional	unemotional

1. Who can read it right? Come on, someone else!
   words plus; negative or positive; shows teacher is in charge; does not specify error; implicit information; discouraging; appeal to other senses; emotional

2. Just look at the sentences again. Then, turn and look at me and say what you remember—I'm only interested in the meaning.

3. Than, than, than and plural—come on, pay attention!

4. I can't believe this.

5. [Draws a line under *than* and under the *s* in *costs*]

6. Say the meaning in your own words.

7a. Look at the board and tell me if I am saying the words on the board right.

   b. This stamp is more expensive the other one. Right? Wrong?

   c. [Student says: You left out *than*—more expensive *than*.]

   d. It costs 15 cent. The other one costs only 3 cent.

   e. [Another student says: Plural, Plural!]

Part Two ■ 173

8a. I'd like each of you to write the sentences as you heard them said just now.

b. Then, compare what you write with the board and make any changes necessary so that they are the same.

9. How many stamps are in the picture?

10. Underline the words that show a comparison is being made.

11. Write down the letter on the stamps that is at the end of the words between the numbers. [The only word between the numbers 15 and 3 is the word *cents*. Just as the word *cents* appears between numbers on some of the stamps in this book.]

Thinking about the Alternatives

Here are the features other people attributed to a few of the instances of feedback provided during the reading lesson.

2. *words plus—seemingly patient tone of voice; teacher in charge, but not as clearly showing this fact as in 1 or 3 or 4; emotional—others do not seem to fit*

5. *nonwords, informative, specified error, and perhaps explicit information*

10. *words, information, teacher in charge, explicit—mentioning comparison, appeals to the eye, unemotional*

Usually characteristics fit to a certain extent, but not in a clear-cut way. But applying the characteristics does cause us to consider different meanings of the features—as well as what meanings the instances of feedback provide to students. In short, the matching provides opportunities to see "[how language] is populated—overpopulated—with the intentions of others." (Bakhtin, 1981, p. 294)

STARTING CLASS

Activity 2A: Disadvantages and Advantages/Likes and Dislikes

There are other ways to become conscious of alternative perceptions of the same teaching practices. One is to write down disadvantages of practices we think are advantageous and positive, and vice versa. Another is to try things we don't like.

Asking a few students for a disadvantage or an advantage of a teaching practice may trigger a wide range of disadvantages and advantages because sometimes student perspectives are quite different from teacher perspectives.

In order to make more explicit your perceptions or beliefs about another step in starting class—taking attendance—you can write some disadvantages and advantages of calling the roll in different ways. One way to take attendance is to require students to indicate their presence with a word such as "Here!" The content of such a response we might call "procedure" or "red tape" or simply "attendance."

Another option is to ask students to indicate their presence by saying something about their personal tastes—what desserts they like, what music they enjoy, people they consider heroes. When students respond with such information, we could call the content of their responses "personal tastes plus procedure." If students were asked to indicate knowledge of some academic material to indicate that they were present, then we might call the content of their response "content plus procedure."

If you think the idea of asking students to respond to the roll by stating some personal information—"personal plus procedure"—or by indicating knowledge of some academic material—"content plus procedure"—is positive, write down two disadvantages of the practice, below. If, on the other hand, you think the practice is negative, write down two possible advantages of the practice, below.

_____
_____
_____
_____
_____

Thinking about Alternative Perspectives

Here are some disadvantages other teachers wrote:

> Students are embarrassed to share personal information; they might like people or music others find strange.

> Students who have to be alert to answer some questions about the academic material that was covered in class might get nervous during the calling of the roll. These few minutes provide the only time for some students to escape, feel relaxed during a class.

Some advantages noted by those who considered the practices negative include:

The tedium of saying "here" five times per week for thirty weeks could be broken by having students say something such as "angel food cake, hot fudge and ice cream."

Students and teachers would learn something about each other that might be referred to in other parts of the class.

Some students who rarely respond to questions would be given a chance to, since each student in the class is called on during the taking of attendance.

Attendance takes little real time. Consequently, it may seem to some inconsequential. But just as disadvantages of practices you consider positive and advantages of practices you consider negative can make your beliefs both conscious and more explicit, and perhaps alter your perception as a result, so the powerful impact the taking of attendance can have must be considered. This is especially the case if we think the impact of the taking of attendance is weak.

Thinking about the Possibilities

Listed below are some ways other teachers have taken the roll. On the blank lines next to each practice, write an *l* for *like*, if you like the practice, and a *dl* for *don't like*, if you object to it in some way.

1. Teacher stands behind desk, looks at students in each row. When there is an empty seat in a row, the teacher bends down and looks at a seating chart on the desk, writes a check mark in a box next to the student's name on the chart. _____

2. Teacher calls each student's surname preceded by "Mr." or "Ms." and expects students to say "Here!" when his or her name is called. When no "Here!" is heard, an absence is noted in the attendance book. From time to time the teacher says, "Speak up; I can't hear you!" and "Not so slow, answer right away." _____

3. Teacher tells students to select a dessert from a list on the blackboard and say the name of the dessert they like best when their name is called. The choices are ice cream, fruit, cake, and pudding. The sentence "I don't like dessert" is also on the blackboard and the teacher says that the sentence is also one of the choices.

    The teacher uses small cards with individual names on them and as she hears a student's response, she writes it on the card.

    Before she begins, she tells the class that each student should write down the names of at least ten students and the dessert choice each states when their names are called. _____

4. As students enter class, they go to a card rack and take out the card with their name on it, sign it, and replace the card in the

rack with the blank side of the card showing, and their signatures obscured. At the end of the period, the teacher notes absent students in the roll book by putting a check mark next to those students whose names are showing in the card rack.
_____

5. Teacher calls students by name and asks them what famous person they want to be called for the next five class sessions. As students respond—Columbus, George Washington, Mishima, Gandhi, Michael Jackson—teacher writes names in roll book next to each student's name. Teacher asks each student to write at least ten student names and the famous names stated by students.
_____

6. On the blackboard the teacher has written these sentences:
   The old man went out to buy some bread.
   It was so late that the bakery had already closed.
Unless the teacher points to the sentences, the students simply answer "here" when their names are called. If the teacher points to either sentence, the student must state one grammatical fact about the sentence in English. For example, the sentences are in the past tense. *Old* is an adjective, *to* is a preposition. Students are asked to say both sentences and write the comments other students make about them.
_____

Activity 2B: Trying What You Don't Like

Select one of the methods you did not like in the preceding activity and try it in your class. Be sure to try the practice in more than one class, since it will take some time to become familiar with the steps and to feel comfortable trying a practice you don't like!

Then, on the lines below, write your reactions and the reactions of several students in different classes to the alternative practice.

_____
_____
_____
_____
_____
_____
_____
_____
_____

BIBLIOGRAPHY

I have divided the readings, which include but go beyond the works referred to in this book, into two categories: those that explore alternative views of reality and those that deal explicitly with the exploration of the reality of teaching.

I can think of few more stimulating ways to begin to understand how we selectively view the reality we daily observe than reading people like these who explore alternative views of reality: Alinksy's activist ideas on social change, the psychologist Arnheim on visual thinking, the anthropologist/ecologist Bateson raising significant issues in all fields. Then there is the historian Boswell tracing the history of intolerance and our mistrust of the different, the historian Eisler suggesting a very different future, the biologist Gould on the misuse of test results, the anthropologist McDermott on the positive effect that seemingly negative classroom behaviors can have, and the mystery writer Simenon on the distortions we all engage in daily.

In my own teaching and work with other teachers, I have been given new enthusiasm to continue by reading the likes of Barnes and Haber and their systematic study of group work, Jackson and his insights into day-to-day teaching, Lortie's explanations for the stability of teaching practices, and Smith's stimulating arguments about the reading process.

None of these authors in either group concentrates on teaching practices; yet their ideas cannot but affect our beliefs, which in turn will affect our practices. Other materials cited do deal directly with practices, as their titles suggest. Of course, as I have never failed to point out in this book, the ways we group our thoughts and materials need to be constantly played with. Boswell, in the introduction to his history of intolerance, reminds us of this fact. He states so clearly the type of spirit we need as we engage in any exploration, whether in books or in our practices, that I have quoted extensively from it here:

> Tracing the course of intolerance reveals much about the landscape it traverses, and for this reason alone it deserves to be studied. . . . Later generations will certainly recognize many wrong turns, false leads, and dead ends mistakenly pursued by those who had no trails to follow, whose only landmarks were those they themselves posted. Once the terrain has been better mapped, it will be possible to improve initial surveys very substantially; early studies may appear in retrospect absurdly roundabout or wholly useless. To this ineluctable hazard of early research is added the difficulty in the case at issue that a great many people believe they already know where the trails *ought* to lead, and they will blame the investigator not only for the inevitable errors of first explorations but also for the extent to which his results, however tentative and well intentioned, do not accord with their preconceptions on the subject. Of such

critics the writer can ask only that before condemning too harshly the placement of his signposts they first experience for themselves the difficulty of the terrain.

(Boswell, 1980, pp. 38, 39)

The strings of numbers and letters after the entries are the Library of Congress or Dewey call numbers. In libraries with open stacks, with the call numbers in hand, one can save a trip to the card catalog or computer terminal and thus have more time to both find the item in question and browse. The asterisk at the end of some entries simply indicates that the author was cited in this book.

*E*XPLORING ALTERNATIVE VIEWS OF REALITY

Alinsky, Saul D. 1971. *Rules for radicals*. New York: Random House.* HN65.A675
Arnheim, Rudolf. 1969. *Visual thinking*. Berkeley: Univ. of California Press* N70.A693
Bakhtin, M. M. 1981. *The dialogic imagination*. Austin: Univ. of Texas Press.* PN3331.B2513 801'.953
Bateson, Gregory. 1972. *Steps to an ecology of mind*. New York: Ballantine.* GN6.B3 504.B78
Bateson, Gregory, and Mary Catherine Bateson. 1988. *Where angels fear*. New York: Bantam.* B72.B37 1988 100
Blake, William. 1863. *Auguries of innocence*. In *The Portable Blake* edited by Alfred Kazin. 1969. New York: Viking.* PR4142.K3 1969
Boswell, John. 1980. *Christianity, social tolerance and homosexuality*. Chicago: Univ. of Chicago Press. HQ76.3E8B67 301.41'57'094
Bronowski, Jacob. 1956. *Science and human values*. New York: Harper and Row.* Q171.B8785 503.B78
Cervantes Saavedra, Miguel de. *Don Quixote*. Chicago: Encyclopaedia Britannica, Inc. pt. 1, chap. 2; pt. 1, chap. 8.* 1952
Eisler, Riane. 1988. *The chalice and the blade—Our history, our future*. San Francisco: Harper and Row. HQ1075.E57 1987 305.3'09
Feynman, Richard P. 1988. *What do you care what other people think?* New York: Bantam.*
Forsyth, Frederick. 1984. *The fourth protocol*. London: Corgi Books.*
Gallwey, Timothy W. 1974. *The inner game of tennis*. New York: Random House.* GV1002.9.P75G34 796.34'2'019
Gardner, John. 1984. *The art of fiction: Notes on craft for young writers*. New York: Knopf. PN 3355.G34 1985
Gleick, James. 1987. *Chaos—Making a new science*. New York: Penguin Books. Q172.5C45G54 1988
Gould, Stephen Jay. 1981. *The mismeasure of man*. New York: Norton. BF431.G68 1981 153.9'3
Hall, Edward T. 1959. *The silent language*. New York: Fawcett. HM258.H3
Kazantzakis, Nikos. 1952. *Zorba the Greek*. New York: Simon and Schuster.*
Michaels, Ian. 1987. *The teaching of English from the sixteenth century to 1870*. Cambridge: Cambridge Univ. Press.* PE65.M5 1987
Plato. 1952. *The dialogues of Plato*. Chicago: Encyclopaedia Britannica, Inc.*
Shah, Idries. 1970. *Tales of the Dervishes*. New York: Dutton.*
Simenon, Georges. 1940. *Maigret on the Riveria*. New York: Harcourt, Brace, Jovanovich.*
Simenon, Georges. 1974. *Maigret and the millionaires*. New York: Harcourt, Brace, Jovanovich.*
Stacey, Michelle. 1989. Profiles: Allen Walker Read. *The New Yorker*, 4 Sept., 51–74.*
Vargas Llosa, Mario. 1986. *Who killed Palomino Molero?* New York: Collier Books.*
Vygotsky, Lev. 1962. *Thought and language*. Cambridge: MIT Press.* P105.V913
Watzlawick, Paul. 1977. *How real is real?* New York: Vintage.* P91W3 301.14
Weiner, Norbert. [1950] 1967. *The human use of human beings, cybernetics and society*. New York: Avon.* Q310.W49 1950

EXPLORING THE REALITY OF TEACHING

Allwright, Dick. 1988. *Observation in the language classroom*. London: Longman. P53.A48 418'.007

Barnes, Douglas. 1976. *From communication to curriculum*. Harmondsworth, Eng.: Penguin.* LB1084.B365 1977

Bellack, Arno et al. 1966. *The language of the classroom*. New York: Teachers College Press. LB 1620.B379

Chaudron, Craig. 1987. *Second language classrooms: Research on teaching and learning*. New York: Cambridge Univ. Press. P54.C43 1987

Edwards, Betty. 1979. *Drawing on the right side of the brain*. Los Angeles: J. P. Tarcher, Inc.* NC730.E34

Fanselow, John F. 1987. *Breaking rules—Generating and exploring alternatives in language teaching*. White Plains, NY: Longman. P51.F36 1987 418.007

Fanselow, John F. 1988. "Let's See": Contrasting conversations about teaching. *TESOL Quarterly* 22, no. 1 (March): 113–130.

Freeman, Donald. 1982. Observing teachers: Three approaches to in-service training and development. *TESOL Quarterly* 16, no. 1 (March): 21–28.

Freire, Paulo. 1970. *Pedagogy of the oppressed*. New York: Continuum.* LB880.F7313

Froebel quoted in Broudy, Harry S. 1965. *Exemplars of teaching method*. Chicago: Rand McNally. page 122.* LA11.B66

Gebhard, Jerry G. 1984. Models of supervision: Choices. *TESOL Quarterly* 18, no. 3 (September): 501–514.

Haber, Steven. 1990. Multiple perspectives of group interaction in an ESL writing class. Dissertation. Teachers College, Columbia University.

Jackson, Philip W. 1968. *Life in classrooms*. New York: Holt, Rinehart and Winston. LB 1032.J3

Jarvis, G. A. 1972. They're tearing up the street where I was born. *Foreign Language Annals* 6, no. 2 (December): 198–205.

Kepler-Zumwalt, Karen, ed. *Improving teaching—1986 ASCD Yearbook*. Alexandria, VA: Association for Supervision and Curriculum Development. LB2804.A8 1986

Liebermann, Anne and Lynne Miller. 1984. *Teachers, their world and their work*. Alexandria, VA: Association for Supervision and Curriculum Development. LB1775.L43 1984

Lier, Leo van. 1988. *The classroom and the language learner*. London: Longman. P53.V36 1988 418'.007

Long, Michael. 1980. Inside the "black box": Methodological issues in classroom research on language learning. *Language Learning* 30: 1–42.

Lortie, Dan C. 1975. *Schoolteacher: A sociological study*. Chicago: Univ. of Chicago Press. LB1775.L56

McDermott, Ray P. 1987. Achieving school failure: An anthropological approach to illiteracy and social stratification. In *Education and cultural process: Anthropological approaches*, 2d ed., ed. George D. Spindler, 173–209. Prospect Heights, IL: Waveland Press. LB45.S64

McDermott, Ray P. 1988. Inarticulateness. In *Linguistics in context*, ed. Deborah Tannen, 123–139. Norwood, NJ: Ablex Publishing. P126.L54 1987

Mehan, Hugh, 1979. *Learning lessons*. Cambridge, MA: Harvard Univ. Press. LB1027.M376

Pak, Janine. 1986. *Find out how you teach—Teacher development*. Adelaide: National Curriculum Resource Centre, Australia.

Richards, Jack, and David Nunan, eds. 1990. *Second language teacher education*. Cambridge: Cambridge Univ. Press. P53.85.S43 1990 418'.0071'1-dc20

Sergiovani, Thomas J., and Robert J. Starratt. 1979. *Supervision: Human perspectives*. New York: McGraw Hill. LB2805.S52 1979

Simon, Anita, and E. Gill Boyer, eds. 1967. *Mirrors for Behavior III: An anthology of observation instruments*. Wyncote, PA: Communication Materials Center.* BF722.M57

Smith, Frank. 1975. *Comprehension and learning*. New York: Holt, Rinehart and Winston.* LB1051.S6218 370.15'2

Smith, Frank. 1978. *Understanding reading*. 2d ed. New York: Holt, Rinehart and Winston.* LB1050.S574 1978 428'.4

STAMPS

1

2

3

4

5

6

182 ■ Stamps

7

8

9

10

11

12

13

Stamps ■ 183